ROUTLEDGE LIBRARY EDITIONS: HUMAN RESOURCE MANAGEMENT

Volume 38

THE SHORTER WORKING WEEK

THE SHORTER WORKING WEEK
With Special Reference to the Two-Shift System

H. M. VERNON

LONDON AND NEW YORK

First published in 1934 by George Routledge & Sons, Ltd.

This edition first published in 2017
by Routledge
2 Park Square, Milton Park, Abingdon, Oxon OX14 4RN

and by Routledge
711 Third Avenue, New York, NY 10017

Routledge is an imprint of the Taylor & Francis Group, an informa business

© 1934 H. M. Vernon

All rights reserved. No part of this book may be reprinted or reproduced or utilised in any form or by any electronic, mechanical, or other means, now known or hereafter invented, including photocopying and recording, or in any information storage or retrieval system, without permission in writing from the publishers.

Trademark notice: Product or corporate names may be trademarks or registered trademarks, and are used only for identification and explanation without intent to infringe.

British Library Cataloguing in Publication Data
A catalogue record for this book is available from the British Library

ISBN: 978-1-138-80870-6 (Set)
ISBN: 978-1-315-18006-9 (Set) (ebk)
ISBN: 978-1-138-28840-9 (Volume 38) (hbk)
ISBN: 978-1-138-28843-0 (Volume 38) (pbk)
ISBN: 978-1-315-26790-6 (Volume 38) (ebk)

Publisher's Note
The publisher has gone to great lengths to ensure the quality of this reprint but points out that some imperfections in the original copies may be apparent.

Disclaimer
The publisher has made every effort to trace copyright holders and would welcome correspondence from those they have been unable to trace.

THE SHORTER WORKING WEEK

WITH SPECIAL REFERENCE TO THE TWO-SHIFT SYSTEM

BY

H. M. VERNON
M.A., M.D.

LONDON
GEORGE ROUTLEDGE & SONS, LTD.
BROADWAY HOUSE: 68–74 CARTER LANE, E.C.
1934

PRINTED IN GREAT BRITAIN BY
MACKAYS LIMITED, CHATHAM

PREFACE

IN 1931 the International Association for Social Progress decided to undertake an enquiry concerning the effects of a shorter working week on unemployment, and the Committee of Enquiry of the British Section of the Association —of which I was a member—published a Report on *New Aspects of the Problem of Hours of Work* in the summer of 1933. As the subject is such a large one, and is changing and developing so rapidly, it seemed to me that it would be helpful if I, in my private capacity, collected further information when opportunity offered, and when I had the necessary leisure for the purpose. The information obtained is embodied in this volume.

H. M. VERNON.

May, 1934.

CONTENTS

                                                                                   PAGE

CHAPTER I.—THE REASONS FOR A REDUCTION IN THE HOURS OF WORK 1

    Introduction—The Curse of Unemployment—The Extent of Unemployment—Short Time—The Increasing Productivity of Labour.

CHAPTER II.—RATIONALISATION. 19

    Introduction — Scientific Management — Vocational Selection and Training—Standardisation—Mass Production—Industrial Combinations—Distribution—Technocracy—The Changes of Employment associated with Rationalisation.

CHAPTER III.—THE WEEKLY HOURS NOW WORKED 44

    Introduction—Hours of Work in Individual Industries in Great Britain—Hours of Work in Certain Unregulated Occupations in Great Britain—Hours of Work in Other Countries—The Five-Day Week—Various Schemes for the Temporary Reduction in Hours of Work—The Working Week of Forty Hours or Less—Overhead Costs—Shift Systems.

CHAPTER IV.—THE TWO-SHIFT SYSTEM . . . 77

    Introduction—The Procedure Adopted in Granting Two-Shift Orders—The Numbers of Orders Granted and Workers Involved—The Reasons for Obtaining Orders—The Hours of Work.

CHAPTER V.—THE TWO-SHIFT SYSTEM IN CONTINUOUS OPERATION 99

    Introduction—Factories Employing the Two-Shift System on a Substantial Scale—Output and Loss of Working Time—The Dependence of Rate of Production on Hours of Work—The Wages Paid—The Influence of the Two-Shift System on Health—The Influence of the Three-Shift System on Health.

CONTENTS

CHAPTER VI.—THE TWO-SHIFT SYSTEM IN INTERMITTENT OPERATION 132

Seasonal Employment—Intermittent Employment not Related to Season—The Administration of Orders used Intermittently—The Occupations for which Orders have been Obtained—The Two-Shift System in Other Countries—The Employment of Boys on the Two-Shift System—Lighting, Heating and Ventilation under the Two-Shift System.

CHAPTER VII.—THE OPINIONS OF THE WORKERS AND OTHERS ON THE TWO-SHIFT SYSTEM . 146

The Opinions of the Workers—Labour Turnover—The Opinions of Managers, Supervisors, and Parents—The Opinions of Workers' Organisations—Opinions Expressed in Parliament—General Conclusions.

CHAPTER VIII.—THE PROBLEM OF LEISURE . . 167

Introduction—Evidence of the Use to which Leisure Hours are Put—The Best Use of Leisure—Leisure and the Two-Shift System—Leisure and the Unemployed—How Other Countries Meet the Problem of Leisure—General Conclusions.

INDEX 197

THE SHORTER WORKING WEEK

CHAPTER I

THE REASONS FOR A REDUCTION IN THE HOURS OF WORK

CONTENTS

Introduction—The Curse of Unemployment—The Extent of Unemployment—Short Time—The Increasing Productivity of Labour

INTRODUCTION

DURING the last few years a more and more insistent demand has arisen for a reduction in the hours of work in industry. The main reason for this demand is the rapid growth of unemployment in most of the industrial countries of the world, coupled with the realisation that this unemployment is due, at least in part, to the great rise in the productivity of labour. Owing to increasing standardisation, the use of machinery, and the application of scientific advances to industrial practice, the output per person has increased so rapidly during the last few years that even if trade revived to its previous maximum degree of prosperity, it is probable that it would be unable to absorb a considerable proportion of the workers now living in a condition of unemployment.

The remedy most frequently suggested is to reduce the hours of work of those now in employment, and thereby to make possible a distribution of the available supply of work over a larger number of individuals; but this remedy, though apparently a simple and straightforward one, is so involved with the economic question of the wages to be paid for these reduced hours of work, that it has proved in practice the reverse of simple. The economic factor is the stumbling-block against which almost all of the suggested schemes for reducing unemployment come to grief, and these schemes are inevitably condemned if they cannot surmount it. It will, therefore, be necessary at all times to bear in mind the immediate practicability of any scheme under consideration. However promising its ultimate practicability, it is useless to discuss it in detail if it cannot be shown that it is applicable to present-day conditions, subject to a reasonable amount of give and take on the part of the rival forces concerned in its adoption.

THE CURSE OF UNEMPLOYMENT

The subject of unemployment is referred to so frequently in our daily Press that it is apt to create the feeling that the evil is unavoidable. Regularly-employed persons who have no personal fear of being forced to join the unemployed classes tend to forget or ignore the tragic conditions which chronic unemployment almost inevitably induces. It is well, therefore, that the subject should be discussed from time to time by public men speaking with authority, for the deeper the realisation of the tragedy the more likely are we to be stimulated to do what we can to abate it. A recent manifesto by the Archbishop of York puts the position of the unemployed so forcibly that it is worth while to reproduce some of his arguments.[1]

The Archbishop pointed out that unemployment is more than a misfortune for those who are overtaken by it; it is a curse. Its chief evil does not consist in the state of physical want which it involves, though that is bad enough. Men can face physical hardship even when it afflicts their wives and children as well as themselves, if they feel that they are serving some cause by enduring it.

---

[1] *The Times*, Jan. 23rd, 1934.

What saps a man's moral strength and fills him with depression, and often with bitterness, is not the physical want; it is the sense that society has no need of him. Unemployment is both an affront and a corrosive poison to his personality. And for the infliction of that insult and injury we are all guilty so far as we acquiesce in an ordering of life which has this consequence. We cannot be content with the present manifestly unjust incidence of reduction in the demand for human labour, whether caused by the introduction of machinery or by general trade depression. The community is at fault in permitting the effects of such changes to fall so unequally as to turn some of its members into a class apart—the unemployed. Our first need and duty is to reach a new attitude of mind with regard to unemployed persons and to the condition of unemployment itself.

It was further pointed out that all the misery and degradation caused by unemployment is permitted to continue in a world where the power of producing wealth is beyond that of all former generations. Man has, through most of his existence, been under the necessity of expending the greater part of his time and energy in obtaining the bare means of subsistence. This is no longer true. There must be something grievously wrong with a society in which, while multitudes are suffering from under-nourishment, food is being burnt and thrown into the sea for lack of a market. The increased leisure made possible by technical progress could and ought to be pure gain. There are talents and capacities in wage-earners for which the work done for wages affords no scope. The unemployed, if given opportunity, may create fresh values for themselves and for the society of which they are members.

The Archbishop laid special stress on the widespread juvenile unemployment, which he regarded as calamitous and indefensible. He pointed out that the arguments for raising the school age advanced by the Hadow Committee, have been endorsed by practical educationists. To send children into industry at 14 is a course open at all times to the gravest objections. The increase in the ranks of young persons from 14 to 18 which will take place during the next three years is likely to be disastrous both to the individual boys and girls concerned, as well as to the national welfare. It is, therefore, urged most strongly that the school age should be immediately raised to 15, or to such later age as may be practicable, and that the proposals in the Unemployment Insurance Bill relating to the provision of authorised courses of training for unemployed persons under 18 years of age should be supported.

It will be generally agreed that the school-leaving age ought to be raised to 15, or, still better, to 16. The practical difficulty lies, not only in the expense of providing additional school accommodation, but in the demand that the children should receive a weekly payment to provide for their maintenance. Many parents have come to expect that their children, when they reach the age of 14, should add substantially to the family budget by means of their earnings, and they are very reluctant to forgo this assistance. It certainly seems reasonable that a small weekly allowance should be made, though a comprehensive system of family endowment would be preferable.

THE EXTENT OF UNEMPLOYMENT

A valuable conspectus of the unemployment problem was published by the International Labour Office at Geneva, in January, 1933, under the title *Hours of Work and Unemployment*. This report is drawn upon frequently in succeeding pages, while more up-to-date information has been obtained from the *Ministry of Labour Gazette*, and elsewhere. The present table summarises the

PERCENTAGE OF INDUSTRIAL WORKERS UNEMPLOYED

Country.	Persons Unemployed.	1925.	1926.	1927.	1928.	1929.	1930.	1931.	1932.	Number of Unemployed in 1931.
Australia	wholly	8·9	7·1	7·0	10·8	11·1	19·3	27·4	(29·2)	117,866
Belgium {	wholly	1·5	1·5	1·8	0·9	1·3	3·6	10·9	(19·3)	79,186
	intermittently	4·5	2·7	3·9	3·5	3·0	7·9	16·9	(21·7)	121,890
Canada	wholly	7·0	5·1	4·9	4·5	5·7	11·1	16·8	(21·4)	33,625
Czechoslovakia	wholly	—	3·0	1·6	1·4	2·2	4·6	8·3	(13·2)	102,179
Denmark	wholly	14·7	20·7	22·5	18·5	15·5	13·7	17·9	(30·5)	53,019
Germany {	wholly	6·7	18·0	8·7	8·6	13·2	22·2	34·3	(43·8)	1,444,845
	partially	10·0	16·0	3·4	5·7	7·5	13·4	20·0	(22·7)	842,357
Great Britain and North Ireland {	wholly	—	8·9	7·5	8·3	8·3	12·0	17·0	(17·6)	2,129,359
	intermittently	—	3·7	2·3	2·6	2·2	4·3	4·7	(4·6)	587,494
Japan	wholly	—	—	—	—	—	5·2	5·9	(6·9)	413,248
Netherlands	wholly	9·6	8·7	9·0	6·9	8·0	9·7	18·2	(29·9)	87,659
Norway	wholly	13·2	24·3	25·4	19·1	15·4	16·6	24·4	(28·9)	11,115
Sweden	wholly	11·0	12·2	12·0	10·6	10·2	11·9	16·8	(21·2)	64,815
Switzerland {	wholly	—	3·4	2·7	2·1	1·8	3·4	5·9	(8·1)	22,092
	intermittently	—	3·9	2·0	1·1	1·7	7·2	12·1	(12·7)	45,100
United States	wholly	—	—	—	13·1	11·9	21·2	26·3	(31·4)	—

numerous tables of unemployment data recorded in the report, and shows the percentages of unemployed persons in various countries from 1925 onwards. The 1932 data are put in brackets, as they relate only to the first nine or ten months of the year. The figures were mostly derived either from trade union returns or from unemployment insurance statistics, and they are not at all closely comparable, as the criteria of unemployment and the method of collecting the information differed so greatly in the different countries. In some countries the unemployed are split up into " wholly unemployed," on the one hand, and " intermittently unemployed," " partially unemployed," or " temporarily stopped," on the other hand, while in other countries all the unemployed are grouped together. Even then the term " unemployed " has very different connotations. Some of the tables in the report record both the number of unemployed shown by trade union or insurance returns, and the number who registered at the employment exchanges; these two numbers often differ enormously. In Czechoslovakia the latter number is nearly three times larger than the former, and in Canada and Germany it is twice as great. The numbers of unemployed recorded in the last column of the table are those obtained from trade union or insurance statistics for the year 1931.

Whatever the system adopted for classifying unemployment, the data in the table, some of which are plotted out in Fig. 1, agree in showing that there was a rapid rise in the percentage of unemployment in all countries from 1930 onwards. The most recently available information indicates that this rise is still continuing in some countries, though it has fortunately shown a regression in our own country. The monthly percentage of unemployed in Great Britain in the years 1930, 1932 and 1933[1] is plotted in Fig. 2, and it will be seen that while the rise of

[1] *Ministry of Labour Gazette,* Jan., 1934.

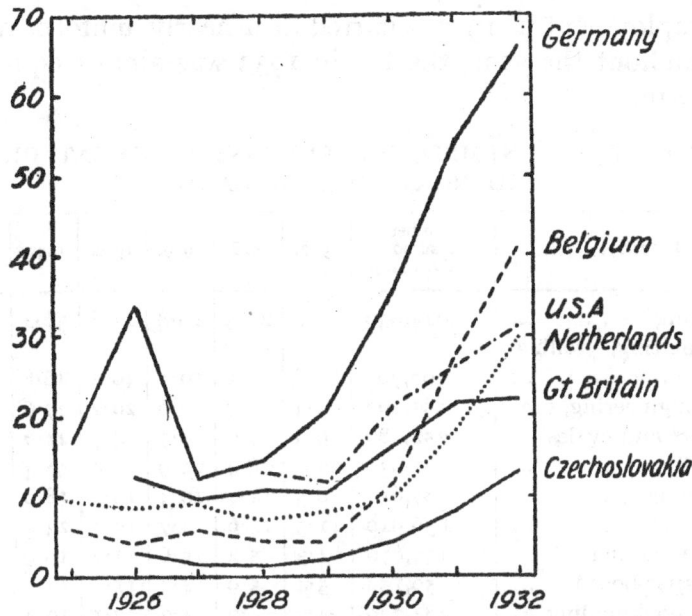

FIG. 1.—Percentage of industrial workers unemployed in various countries.

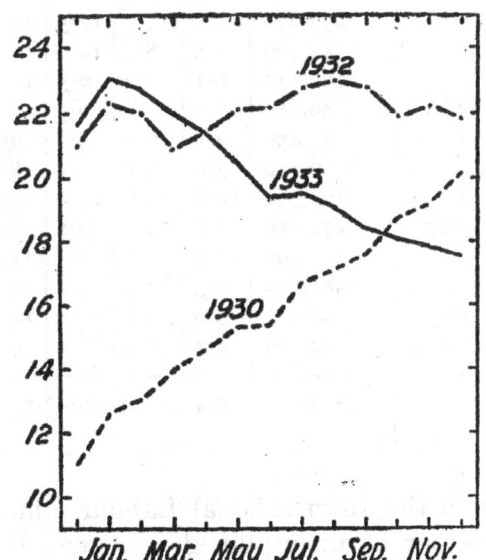

FIG. 2.—Monthly variations of unemployment in Great Britain.

8 THE SHORTER WORKING WEEK

unemployment in 1930 occurred at a nearly uniform rate throughout the year, the fall in 1933 was almost equally uniform.

PERCENTAGE OF UNEMPLOYED PERSONS IN GREAT BRITAIN AND NORTHERN IRELAND

Industry.	Number insured (July, 1932).	1927.	1928.	1929.	1930.	1931.	1932.
Coal-mining	1,044,830	18·2	22·4	16·8	21·8	30·4	(35·5)
Steel smelting, rolling, etc.	167,760	19·8	20·2	20·7	40·2	46·8	(47·3)
General engineering, etc.	551,200	9·4	9·7	9·6	20·2	27·6	(29·0)
Motor-cars and cycles	252,080	6·3	7·2	6·7	14·7	21·7	(20·6)
Shipbuilding	181,930	22·2	28·4	22·9	37·9	58·4	(61·8)
Brickmaking	87,650	8·5	11·7	10·4	15·2	18·0	(22·2)
Building	856,910	11·5	12·6	12·7	17·7	23·4	(28·0)
Furniture-making	133,870	4·3	5·2	5·6	11·7	16·9	(20·2)
Paper, paper-board	59,150	5·4	3·9	4·2	11·5	12·2	(11·5)
Printing, bookbinding	284,770	4·3	4·0	4·2	7·1	10·3	(10·5)
Cotton trade	517,950	8·5	12·0	14·1	44·5	33·9	(30·2)
Tailoring	211,660	6·5	7·8	7·8	12·1	14·2	(14·4)
Boots and shoes	137,970	6·6	15·1	12·5	21·8	19·8	(20·8)
Leather: tanning	42,480	6·5	8·3	10·6	15·0	17·4	(16·7)
Chemicals	99,120	6·1	6·2	6·5	14·9	18·6	(16·6)
Bread, biscuits, cake	159,250	6·0	6·8	6·5	10·4	12·3	(11·8)
Railway service	134,450	4·8	6·4	5·5	9·0	12·2	(16·2)
Tramways, omnibus	180,510	3·0	3·1	3·1	4·3	5·4	(5·9)
Shipping service	161,330	16·1	16·9	17·9	27·3	30·2	(33·0)
Gas, water, etc., supply	174,210	5·0	5·9	6·1	7·8	9·2	(11·0)
Local Government	339,790	7·9	9·1	9·3	11·5	14·9	(18·2)
Hotels, etc.	381,930	7·5	8·5	9·2	14·8	18·1	(16·5)
Entertainments, sports	97,530	9·0	10·1	11·8	18·4	21·6	(20·3)
Professional services	137,160	2·5	2·7	3·2	4·4	5·7	(6·3)
All insured trades	12,808,000	9·4	11·0	10·4	17·8	21·1	(21·9)

According to the International Labour Office bulletin, the total number of unemployed in Great Britain and Northern Ireland was 2,308,779 in December, 1933, as against 2,849,025 in December, 1932.[1] In Germany, the relative improvement was greater, the numbers being 3,714,107 and 5,355,428 at the dates mentioned. Austria, Australia and Canada showed smaller improvements, while unemployment was more severe in the autumn of 1933 than in 1932 in Bulgaria, Czechoslovakia, New Zealand, Norway and Poland.

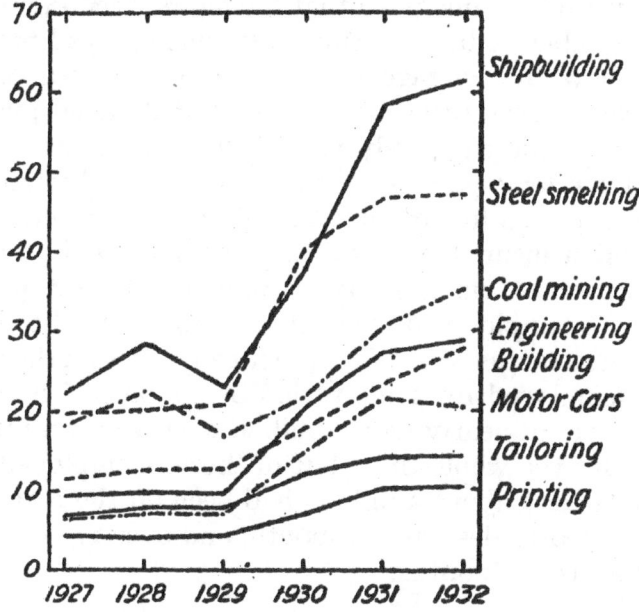

Fig. 3.—Percentage of unemployed in various industries (Great Britain).

The I.L.O. Report gives details of the unemployment in various industries for a number of countries, and the figures for Great Britain and Northern Ireland are reproduced, in a condensed form, in the accompanying table. It will be seen that the extent of unemployment varied very greatly even in 1927 to 1929, the extreme range being from 28·4 per cent. in shipbuilding to 2·5 per cent. in "professional services." Some of the data are plotted in Fig. 3, and it will be seen from these curves, and from the

[1] *The Times*, Jan. 6th, 1934.

other data in the table, that almost all the industries showed a considerable rise between 1929 and 1930. The majority showed further rises in 1931 and 1932, but a few reached their peak in 1930. Shipbuilding was the most severely affected of all the industries, its employment figure in the first nine months of 1932 (which is as far as the data extend) being no less than 61·8 per cent.

It must not be imagined that the figures recorded in the last two tables indicate permanently unemployed persons. They show the average number of unemployed on the days when the returns were made, but detailed analysis shows that comparatively few of the workers are unemployed for long periods of time. In Great Britain, for instance, it was found[1] that though 2½ million out of the 12½ million insured persons were unemployed in 1932-3, on an average, no less than 6 million different persons claimed unemployment benefit or transitional benefit in the course of the year, *i.e.*, practically every other man was unemployed for some period or periods. There was a hard core of nearly half a million men who were unemployed for the whole time, but of those unemployed on a particular day about a million had been on the register of unemployed for less than a month, and over 1,300,000 for less than three months.

SHORT TIME

In most countries, if not in all of them, a considerable proportion of the employed workers are on short time, and therefore earn substantially less than the full-wage rate. The table on p. 11 shows the extent of short time in Great Britain in a few typical industries for the week ending October 24th, 1931.[2]

It will be seen that in several industries from a third to

[1] Dale, J. A., *Journ. Roy. Statist. Soc.*, Jan., 1934.
[2] *Ministry of Labour Gazette*, 1933, pp. 9, 45 and 83.

THE REASONS FOR REDUCTION

a quarter of the workpeople were on short time, while in others the proportion was 2 per cent. or less. The short-timers lost, on an average, about 11 hours per week, so it

SHORT TIME IN BRITISH INDUSTRIES IN 1931

Industry.	Number of workpeople concerned.	Percentage of workers on short time.	Hours of short time per week.
Bleaching, printing, dyeing	75,760	35·8	14·9
Pottery	47,005	27·3	15·3
Boots and shoes	86,529	26·1	9·7
Smelting, rolling, steel, etc.	75,106	24·9	15·3
Engineering, etc.	540,999	22·4	10·9
Woollen and worsted	169,893	20·6	11·8
Chemical	55,431	11·9	7·5
Cotton	298,284	11·5	16·2
Brick, tile, etc.	53,336	9·1	13·0
Printing, bookbinding	93,275	7·7	10·3
Building	241,558	2·0	10·9
Bread-baking	44,021	1·5	7·9

follows that—on the normal 48-hour basis—they were employed only about 37 hours a week.

A few later data, for the week ending September 24th, 1932, are given in the following table.[1]

Industry.	Number of workpeople employed.	Percentage on short time.	Hours of short time per week.
Pottery	56,796	46	12·5
Boots and shoes	110,352	46	10·5
Woollen and worsted	188,936	27	13
Brick	67,071	16	15
Cotton	379,252	15	17

[1] *Hours of Work and Unemployment*, I.L.O., p. 182, 1933.

It will be seen that in every instance the percentage of workpeople on short time was considerably greater than on the earlier date, though the hours worked were reduced to about the same extent.

Germany.—In some of the other countries short time is considerably more extensive than in Great Britain. For instance, in September, 1932, the trade union members in Germany had only 56·4 per cent. of their number in employment, of whom 33·7 per cent. were on full time and 27·7 per cent. on short time. On an average the short-time workers were employed for 13·7 hours per week less than the normal hours.

America.—In the United States the average weekly hours of work have fallen rapidly since 1929. The data adduced by the Bureau of Labour Statistics,[1] which relate to manufacturing processes in general, show that the hours worked in 1932 were 13·5 less per week than in 1929, and in addition the hourly rate of pay was substantially less. Still, the cost of living fell 22 per cent. between 1929 and 1932, so real wages fell less than these figures suggest.

Date.	Average hours per week.	Average hourly earnings.
1929	48·4	58·9 cents
1930	43·9	58·9 ,,
1931	40·4	56·5 ,,
1932	34·9	49·6 ,,

The average hours of work in individual industries were ascertained independently (in March, 1933) by the National Industrial Conference Board and the Bureau of Labour Statistics from figures supplied voluntarily by various industrial establishments. The two sets of data show a fair correspondence in most instances, and it will be seen from the table on p. 13 that iron and steel production, and the related industries, were most heavily

[1] *Internat. Lab. Rev.* 28, p. 365, 1933.

HOURS OF WORK IN VARIOUS INDUSTRIES (U.S.A.)

Group.	Hours per week.		Group.	Hours per week.	
	Bureau of L.S.	N.I.C.B.		Bureau of L.S.	N.I.C.B.
Cotton goods	44·1	44·8	Printing books	36·4	36·1
Meat-packing	42·3	45·6	Furniture	30·7	29·8
Chemical	40·8	38·2	Machine tools	30·0	28·2
Printing news and magazines	40·6	40·3	Motor-cars	29·0	26·9
Boots and shoes	—	39·4	Agricultural implements	28·9	33·6
Hosiery and knit goods	39·3	35·3	Electrical manufacturing	28·0	30·0
Paper boxes	39·1	40·3	Hardware	28·7	26·6
Wool	37·3	36·9	Iron and steel	25·6	28·1
Silk and rayon	36·9	34·5	Foundries and machine shops	27·7	24·6
			Rubber	24·2	24·3

affected. Even these figures are not so depressing as the following, which show the extent of unemployment and short time among members of the American Federation of Labour in September, 1932.

Group.	Percentage unemployed.	Per cent. of those employed working short time.
Building trades	65	43
Metal trades	46	50
Printing trades	20	50
All other trades	20	26

The average weekly earnings of the workers declined in all industries till 1933, but then a rise began in April. In the summer and autumn a further substantial rise was effected by the action of the National Recovery Administration, working under President Roosevelt's autocratic powers, but exact numerical data of the results achieved are not yet available. It is stated[1] that in March no less than 13,680,000 persons were out of work, and by October, according to the estimate of the American Federation of Labour, this number had fallen to something under 11,000,000. By December it is claimed that the total unemployed were less than 7,000,000, but the accuracy of this figure has been challenged.

THE INCREASING PRODUCTIVITY OF LABOUR

The increasing productivity of labour is one of the most striking phenomena of the present century. Productivity received a special impetus during the war, owing to the need of the largest possible output of munitions and other war material, but the war-time acceleration, so far from showing any signs of falling off in subsequent years, spread rapidly to almost every industry, and in some occupations the production has augmented to an almost incredible extent. For instance, it is stated[2] that while the old-fashioned brickmaker never obtained an average of more than 450 bricks a day, a modern brick-making plant can produce 400,000 bricks a day per employee. This means that 100 men, working five modern brick plants, can to-day manufacture all the bricks that the United States can use. Again, in the glass industry, one Owens machine run by nine workers can produce from 15,000 to 35,000 bottles in 24 hours, and take the place of 80 to 90 manual workers.[3] In the manufacture of electric light bulbs (40 watts) semi-automatic machines have a production rate 2·2 times greater than that of hand labour, while automatic machines of various types have one which is 15 to 31 times greater.[4]

America.—Spectacular improvements such as those mentioned do not apply to the majority of manufactured

---

[1] *The Times*, Dec. 27th, 1933.
[2] *Op. cit.*, Jan. 5th, 1933.
[3] *Hours of Work and Unemployment*, p. 16.
[4] *Bulletin of U.S. Bureau of Labour Statistics*, July, 1927.

THE REASONS FOR REDUCTION

articles, but it is stated[1] that between 1920 and 1929 industry as a whole in the United States increased its manufacturing production 36 per cent., though the number of workers employed in its factories declined 6 per cent. Striking as these figures appear, their gravity may be even better realised if we accept the statement that they indicate that "barely half the present army of unemployed, now calculated to embrace a quarter of the entire working population, would be re-absorbed in industry even if the American factories resumed their peak production of 1929." Another estimate[2] asserts that "the adult population of this nation would need to work only four hours a day and four days a week to supply all their material wants."

More detailed information concerning production is given in the report of the I.L.O.[3] One of its tables is here reproduced in modified form, and it will be seen that it

PRODUCTION IN THE UNITED STATES

Industry.	Number of workers.		Percentage increase in 1927.	
	1919.	1927.	Output.	Output per worker.
Agriculture	11,300,000	10,400,000	19	29·5
Mining	1,050,000	1,050,000	40	40·5
Manufactures	10,686,000	9,868,000	30·5	42·5
Railway transport	1,913,000	1,737,000	2·5	12·5
Total or average	24,949,000	23,055,000	24·5	35

indicates a substantial falling off in the number of persons employed in the U.S.A. between the years 1919 and 1927. Yet the total output went up 24·5 per cent. on an average, and the output per person went up 35 per cent. The improvement was greatest in mining and in manufactures,

[1] *The Times*, Jan. 5th, 1933.
[2] *The Observer*, Jan. 8th, 1933.
[3] *Hours of Work and Unemployment*, pp. 168–176.

but it will be noted that agriculture likewise showed a marked improvement.

The table below, drawn from the same source, shows the rise of man-hour productivity in certain industries over a period of 28 years. It will be seen from this table, and from the results plotted in Fig. 4, that in several industries

MAN-HOUR PRODUCTIVITY IN CERTAIN INDUSTRIES (U.S.A.)

Year.	Iron and steel.	Motor-cars.	Boots and shoes.	Petroleum refining.	Paper and pulp.	Flour milling.	Slaughtering and meat-packing.
1899	59	—	100	61	—	—	—
1904	69	40	108	57	83	94	—
1909	100	35	100	117	95	92	115
1914	100	100	100	100	100	100	100
1919	100	141	108	97	105	95	98
1921	87	190	111	114	95	118	113
1923	131	265	119	138	117	127	120
1924	130	258	115	165	121	139	125
1925	153	280	115	179	127	143	121
1926	157	302	115	169	136	154	127
1927	155	278	124	182	140	159	126

there was not much rise in production between 1899 (or 1904) and 1919, but that all of them showed a remarkable and persistent increase from 1919 onwards.

Great Britain.—The output figures for Great Britain are much less striking than those for America, but the data in the table on p. 17 show that between 1924 and 1929 there was an increase of 0·8 to 27·1 per cent. in the output per worker in various industries, except in textiles, where there was a reduction of 5·2 per cent. The heavy industries, coal mining and iron and steel production, showed the greatest improvements. Taking all the industries together, there was an improvement of 11·1 per cent. in output in the five years. During this period the average degree of employment remained fairly steady, but it varied greatly in the individual industries. Sometimes

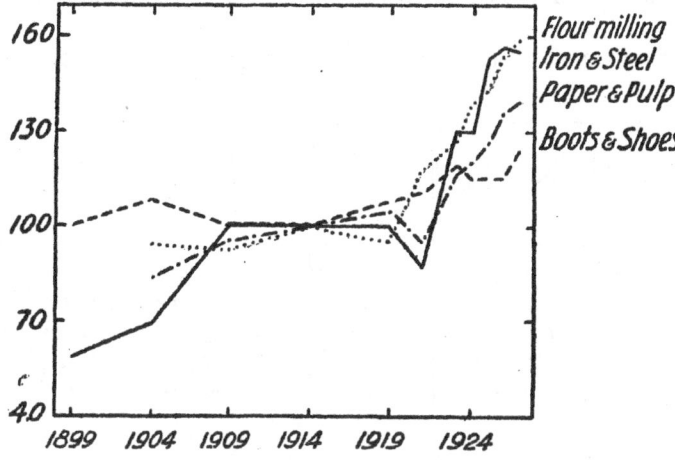

Fig. 4.—The post-war acceleration of productivity in various industries (U.S.A.).

an increase of output was associated with an increase of employment and sometimes with a decrease. There was no sort of consistency.

EMPLOYMENT AND PRODUCTION IN CERTAIN INDUSTRIES (GREAT BRITAIN)

Year.		Coal-mining.	Iron and steel.	Engineering and Ship-building.	Textiles.	Food, drink, tobacco.	Leather and boots.	Chemicals.	All industries.
Relative employment in	1924	100·0	100·0	100·0	100·0	100·0	100·0	100·0	100·0
	1927	76·9	96·2	96·5	106·2	104·4	100·9	104·8	100·2
	1928	70·5	92·9	104·1	104·6	104·1	92·5	110·4	98·7
	1929	75·9	94·5	107·3	103·9	104·6	92·1	111·7	100·6
Relative output per worker in	1924	100·0	100·0	100·0	100·0	100·0	100·0	100·0	100·0
	1927	122·4	114·3	112·2	94·7	95·5	106·7	100·4	106·6
	1928	126·2	110·2	115·7	95·5	97·8	110·4	99·9	106·9
	1929	127·1	120·6	115·6	94·8	101·4	106·9	100·8	111·1

C

Germany.—The relative output per hour of various industrial groups in Germany between the years 1926 and 1931 is shown in the following table. It will be seen that in

RELATIVE PRODUCTION IN CERTAIN INDUSTRIES (GERMANY)

Year.	Mining.	Iron and steel.	Mechanical Engineering.	Building.	Chemicals.	Textiles.	Clothing.	Food.
1926	100·0	100·0	100·0	100·0	100·0	100·0	100·0	100·0
1927	104·3	113·7	102·4	101·1	102·2	107·3	104·2	101·9
1928	111·5	121·2	117·3	108·6	107·5	98·5	108·5	104·5
1929	119·1	124·1	124·6	114·5	112·7	100·6	113·4	107·0
1930–1	117·9	125·0	125·0	115·0	113·0	108·8	110·0	110·0

all of them there was a substantial rise, the improvement during the interval of 4½ years investigated ranging from 10 to 25 per cent.

CHAPTER II

RATIONALISATION

CONTENTS

Introduction—Scientific Management—Vocational Selection and Training—Standardisation—Mass Production—Industrial Combinations—Distribution—Technocracy—The Changes of Employment Associated with Rationalisation

INTRODUCTION

THE increasing productivity of labour is due to a number of causes, most of which have conveniently been grouped under the generic title of "rationalisation." In May, 1927, a World Economic Conference, representing employers, employed and economists, was held at Geneva under the auspices of the League of Nations, and the Industrial Committee of the Conference formulated a series of resolutions which were adopted by the Conference as a whole. They defined the word "rationalisation" in the following terms:

"Rationalisation, by which we understand the methods of technique and of organisation designed to secure the minimum waste of either effort or material. It includes the scientific organisation of labour, standardisation both of material and of products, simplification of processes and improvements in the system of transport and marketing."

The Conference further stated that it "has unanimously recognised the benefits of rationalisation and of scientific management, and it asserts the urgent need of greater, more far-reaching and better co-ordinated efforts in this field." Though conscious of the advantages of rationalisation, the Conference was not "blind to the temporary unfavourable consequences which its application may involve in the case of certain categories of workers. Though, both directly and as consumers, the latter should in due course obtain their share of the advantages of a better organisation of production, they may be adversely affected for a time by temporary unemployment while readjustments are being made."

The Conference summed up their conclusions in a series of resolutions which are so important that it is worth while quoting them in full, in spite of their length.[1]

"The Conference considers that such rationalisation aims simultaneously:

(1) At securing the maximum efficiency of labour with the minimum of effort;
(2) At facilitating by a reduction in the variety of patterns (where such variety offers no obvious advantage) the design, manufacture, use and replacement of standardised parts;
(3) At avoiding waste of raw materials and power:
(4) At simplifying the distribution of goods;
(5) At avoiding in distribution unnecessary transport, burdensome financial charges and the useless interposition of middlemen.

"Its judicious and constant application is calculated to secure:

(1) To the community greater stability and a higher standard in the conditions of life;
(2) To the consumer lower prices and goods more carefully adapted to general requirements;
(3) To the various classes of producers higher and steadier remuneration to be equitably distributed among them.

[1] Cf. "The Social Aspects of Rationalisation," *I.L.O. Studies and Reports, Series B*, No. 18, Geneva, 1931.

" It must be applied with the care which is necessary in order, while at the same time continuing the process of rationalisation, not to injure the legitimate interests of the workers ; and suitable measures should be provided for cases where during the first stage of its realisation it may result in loss of employment or more arduous work.

" It requires, further, so far as regards the organisation of labour in the strict sense of the term the co-operation of employees, and the assistance of trade and industrial organisations and of scientific and technical experts.

" The Conference accordingly recommends that Governments, public institutions, trade and industrial organisations or public opinion as the case may be :

(1) Should lead producers to direct their endeavours along the lines indicated above, and in particular :

(*a*) To encourage and promote in every way the investigation and comparison of the most adequate methods and most practical processes of rationalisation and of scientific management, and of the economic and social results obtained thereby ;

(*b*) To apply these endeavours in industry, agriculture, trade and finance, not merely to large but also to medium and small undertakings, and even to individual workers and handicraftsmen, bearing in mind the favourable effects which they may have in household organisation and amenities ;

(*c*) To give special attention to measures of a kind calculated to ensure to the individual the best, the healthiest and the most worthy employment, such as vocational selection, guidance and training, the due allotment of time between work and leisure, methods of remuneration giving the worker a fair share in the increase of output, and, generally, conditions of work and life favourable to the development and preservation of his personality ;

(2) Should carry on systematically on an international as well as a national basis the standardisation of materials, parts and products of all types which are of international importance, in order to remove the obstacles to production and trade which might arise from a purely national policy of standardisation ;

(3) Should undertake on an international basis investigations for ascertaining the best methods employed and the most conclusive results obtained in every country in the application of the principles set out above, utilising the investigations already made in certain countries and encouraging the exchange of information among those concerned ;

(4) Should spread in all quarters a clear realisation of the advantages and the obligations involved in rationalisation and scientific management as well as of the possibility of their gradual achievement."[1]

It will be realised that the subject of rationalisation is such a huge one that an adequate description of it would need a separate volume. It is maintained,[2] with some justification, that the process of rationalisation involves " a new industrial revolution " ; but nevertheless a brief discussion of some of its main aspects may help to make its relationship to productivity more evident, and thereby to accentuate the argument for a shorter working week in industry.

[1] League of Nations Internat. Economic Conf., Geneva, 1927, *Final Record*, pp. 38–40.
[2] Meakin, W., *The New Industrial Revolution*, London, 1928.

SCIENTIFIC MANAGEMENT

The first and most important steps in the development of rationalisation to obtain wide recognition are identified with the name of F. W. Taylor, an American engineer, who worked out detailed methods of workshop management and organisation. He described some of his experiments at a meeting of the American Society of Mechanical Engineers as early as 1890, and more than twenty years later he embodied his main conclusions in two books entitled *Shop Management* and *The Principles of Scientific Management*.[1] He maintained that the traditional rule-of-thumb methods hitherto adopted in industry ought to be re-examined with the detachment from preconceptions and the integrity to truth of a worker in the exact sciences. When asked to define scientific management he used to say " it is a mental revolution." It could not be defined in terms of method alone; it involved also a new attitude of mind.[2] Taylor's methods apply to the control of a single factory rather than to the wider problems of industry as a whole, so they constitute only a fraction of what we now know as rationalisation.

In the management of a factory or workshop, Taylor pointed out that " what the workmen want from their employers beyond anything else is high wages, and what employers want from their workmen is a low labour cost of manufacture," but he also stressed the fact that " no system or scheme of management should be considered which does not in the long run give satisfaction to both employer and employee."[3] In order to attain these ends, Taylor enumerated a number of objects to be aimed at and the organisation for attaining them. He and his disciple

---

[1] Taylor, F. W., *Shop Management*, New York, 1911, and *The Principles of Scientific Management*, New York, 1915.
[2] Urwick, L., *The Meaning of Rationalisation*, p. 26, 1929.
[3] Taylor, F. W., *Shop Management*, p. 21.

Gilbreth[1] maintained that the " one best way " of performing each piece of work or process should be ascertained by exact time and motion study of the constituent elements of the task, and the combination, into an organic whole, of those which are quickest. This plan for attaining maximum speed by eliminating all unnecessary movements was to be used as a standard by all the workers; but it has to some extent been controverted by Farmer,[2] Myers[3] and other industrial psychologists, who point out that different workers have different methods of performing the same task, and that the sequence of movements involved in performing a task ought to be framed in an easy rhythm with the avoidance of sudden changes of direction.

A few examples of the effects of motion study in accelerating various industrial processes may be quoted. In assembly work, for instance, motion study led to the reduction of the time required to assemble carburettors from 450 to 45 minutes, and to assemble pumps, from 360 to 60 minutes.[4] Experiments at a French printing works showed that time and motion studies on the setting of type for time-tables led to an eightfold increase in the output of type-setting, and a sevenfold reduction in the time required for making corrections. Taking the work altogether, it was found possible to economise in the labour supply by as much as 75 per cent.[5] A group of girls engaged in grinding and polishing spoons and forks showed a reduction of 8 to 61 per cent. in the time required, and another group showed an average reduction of 29 per cent.[6] Girls working in a confectionery factory showed, as the result of motion study, an increase of 88 per cent.

[1] Gilbreth, F. B., *Motion Study*, New York, 1911.
[2] Farmer, E., Report No. 14 of Indust. Fatigue Res. Board, 1921.
[3] Myers, C. S., *Industrial Psychology in Great Britain*, London, 1925.
[4] Gilbreth, L. M., *Journ. Soc. Auto. Eng.*, 17, p. 399, 1925.
[5] Quoted from *The Social Aspects of Rationalisation*, p. 18.
[6] Farmer, E., and Brooke, R., Report No. 15 of Indust. Fatigue Res., 1921.

in their efficiency at chocolate dipping, 50 per cent. in bottling sweets, and 38 per cent. in packing chocolates.[1]

In addition to advice in the method of performing his task, the worker—under Taylor's method—is given an instruction card bearing an exact description of the tools and appliances to be used, and the machine speeds and adjustments. He is set a standard time for each separate element and for the complete task, and if he finishes the work in less than the standard time he may be paid at a higher " differential piece rate." The tools, machines and equipment are kept available for use and in a proper condition by a special staff, and all waste time between successive jobs is eliminated, so far as possible, by systems of planning and routing. The movement of the articles manufactured from machine to machine and from department to department is controlled in detail so as to get the work completed at certain pre-arranged times, whereby the volume of work in progress, and consequently of capital invested, is kept at a minimum.[2]

The rationalisation of movements, when extended to the whole of any labour process, is termed " chain work." In some industries, such as the motor-car industry, an assembling belt-conveyer is used to move on the gradually-evolving car slowly from worker to worker, each of whom is responsible for one small task. The workers form a continuous and unbroken chain, linking one operation with another, until the assembly is complete. In France the Eastern Railway has for some years past used chain work in its workshops for rolling-stock. The time required for fitting brake levers has thereby been reduced from 2·5 to 1·3 hours, and for the inspection of bogies, from 32·1 hours to 18·6 hours. In a French bicycle factory the application of the chain system to the final fitting of the bicycles led to a saving of four-ninths in labour costs, after

[1] Farmer, E., *Journ. Indust. Hyg.*, 4, p. 154, 1922.
[2] *Cf.* Pitman's *Dictionary of Industrial Administration*, p. 761, 1928.

allowing for an increase of 20 per cent. in the wages of each worker. In Germany the time required for fitting Knorr brakes to railway rolling-stock has been reduced from 156 hours to 46 hours, and in the Brandenburg locomotive repair shops a task formerly requiring four months is now done in 15 days. In a motor workshop at Dentz the introduction of chain work reduced the time of manufacture from 1,700 minutes to 500 minutes. A wagon factory in Hanover was able, in two years, to reduce its unproductive expenditure 75 per cent.[1]

To return to Taylor's system, the staff of the factory was radically reorganised. Instead of expecting a foreman of the old-fashioned type to be responsible for carrying out all the new methods of scientific management, Taylor at first installed several " functional foremen," each giving instruction to the workmen in regard to one aspect of their work. This plan introduced a number of difficulties, and is now replaced by a system in which the workmen in each department are under the direction of a single foreman, but the foreman receives his instructions from the members of a staff of functional departments.[2] These departments deal with employment or administration of personnel, design of product, methods and processes to be employed, time study and rate fixing, maintenance of plant and tools, planning and routing of work, storekeeping of material, inspection of quality of work, and other factors.

VOCATIONAL SELECTION AND TRAINING

Taylor's system included the selection of the most suitable workers for the various tasks, and their training in the methods required. In a few instances he used psychological tests for selecting the workers, but the

---

[1] *Social Aspects of Rationalisation*, pp. 20–24.
[2] Pitman's *Dictionary of Industrial Administration*, p. 762.

introduction of systematic methods of vocational guidance and selection is a post-war phenomenon. It is one which is still in an early stage of development, but the success already attained is sufficient to give some idea of the importance it is likely to achieve ultimately. A recently-published book on *Industrial Psychology*[1] devotes nearly 200 pages, or a third of its contents, to a description of what it terms " Fitting the Worker to the Job." It contains chapters dealing with " job analysis," the interview of applicants for work, the standardisation and administration of psychological tests, and detailed descriptions of the application of these tests to young persons entering industry and to skilled and semi-skilled workers.

A few of the many examples adduced by Viteles may be given to show the usefulness of selection tests. (1) When 30 machinist apprentices were divided into three classes according to their ability to perform certain tests, it was found that the third who were best at the tests took 79 hours to complete a number of standard workshop tasks, the middle third took 99 hours, and the worst third, 102 hours. (2) When a group of 262 tool-making apprentices were chosen in the ordinary way without any selection tests, it was found that 61 per cent. of them subsequently proved satisfactory, but of another group of 284 apprentices who were selected by means of tests, 83 per cent. proved satisfactory. (3) When a group of taxi-cab drivers were tested, the men (34 in number) who showed themselves to be " unsatisfactory " at the tests were found to incur accidents five times more frequently than the 258 men found to be " satisfactory." (4) When a fresh group of letter sorters for the U.S. postal service were selected as the result of tests, it was found that 93 per cent. of them were of greater efficiency than the average shown by the sorters chosen on the haphazard system previously in force.

[1] Viteles, M. S., *Industrial Psychology*, London, 1933.

Other information on the selection and training of new employees is summarised by Welch and Miles[1] in their book on *Industrial Psychology in Practice*. (1) It was found that when tests were employed for selecting employees in confectionery manufacture, only 3 per cent. of them proved to be " misfits," *i.e.*, workers who had to be dismissed or transferred to other work. Previous to the use of the tests the misfits were 20 to 25 per cent. (2) At a large electric lamp works the workers in the diamond-piercing department (for making the dies through which the wire filaments are drawn) had to be trained for one or two years at an average cost of £250 per head. The men were recruited from the ordinary factory staff, and 50 per cent. of them were found to be incompetent, but when psychological selection tests were introduced the incompetents fell to 12·5 per cent. (3) In a chocolate factory the training of the new workers took about 18 months and cost the firm over £30, but after the introduction of vocational tests and the reorganisation of the training scheme the training period was reduced to 3½ months, and the cost per worker to less than £5.

STANDARDISATION

Standardisation of the materials employed and of the articles produced plays an important part in rationalisation. The standardisation often includes simplification of processes, patterns and products, and outstanding advances in these directions have been made during the last twenty years, especially in the engineering industry. This is due largely, in this country, to the work of the British Engineering Standards Association, and it has resulted in the establishment and general acceptance of standard dimensions over a wide range of manufactured

[1] Welch, H. J., and Miles, G. H., *Industrial Psychology in Practice*, London, 1932.

articles such as rolled steel sections, angles and beams, and drastic reduction in the number of sizes and patterns. This standardisation is of great advantage in limiting the permissible inaccuracy in dimensions, weight and strength. It greatly reduces the stocks of manufactured articles which have to be maintained, and saves a locking up of capital and a waste of space.

In America standardisation and simplification were greatly stimulated under Mr. Hoover's secretaryship of the Department of Commerce, which was initiated in 1921. Mr. Hoover defined " simplified practice " as " the reduction of variety in sizes, dimensions, and immaterial difference in everyday commodities. Its purpose is to eliminate waste, decrease cost, and increase values in production, distribution, and consumption." Under his stimulus nine hundred conferences had been held by the end of 1925, and four hundred trade groups were engaged in working out schedules of simplified shapes and sizes. These schedules covered thousands of varieties of articles, and a few typical reductions may be quoted. Pocket-knives were reduced from 1,500 to 300 varieties ; hammers and hatchets from 2,752 to 761 ; pipes and fittings from 2,982 to 364 ; spades and shovels from 4,000 to less than 400 ; blankets from 78 to 12.[1] Again, it is stated[2] that the number of types of electric lamps, which was 55,000 in 1900, was reduced to 342 in 1923 by the standardisation of voltages and caps.

In Germany, standardisation and simplification have a long history under the Reichskuratorium für Wirtschaftlichkeit (German Federal Board of Efficiency). This is a State Institution which studies rationalisation in all its forms, and endeavours to promote its application throughout industry.[3] A striking example of the results achieved

[1] Meakin, W., *The New Industrial Revolution*, p. 153, 1928.
[2] *Standards Year Book*, p. 17, 1930.
[3] *Bulletin of Internat. Management Inst.*, Geneva, Jan., 1933, p. 1.

is found in the motor-car industry, where the number of lines was reduced from 146 to 40 between 1924 and 1927. In Czechoslovakia[1] the number of types of railway rails was reduced from 43 to 7, of screws from 2,300 to 220, and of belts from 3,600 to 600.

In Great Britain standardisation has been developed in such industries as paper-making as well as in the engineering and metal trades, and a committee has recently been established by the President of the Board of Trade to stimulate the growth of standardisation and simplification throughout the country.[2]

MASS PRODUCTION

This term implies the production of articles in very large quantities by repetition processes, and though the method has been used in a number of industries for a number of years, it is assigned in popular estimation more especially to the engineering and metal industries. During the war the mass production of shells, cartridges and other munitions reached an almost incredible height, millions of men and women being employed in their manufacture by day and by night. Since the war mass production has been extended to many industries which knew little of it in pre-war times, but the engineering and metal trades still retain their pre-eminence in applying it. Of engineering trades, the motor-car industry is the most outstanding example. It owes its mass production methods particularly to Henry Ford, but the American methods have been successfully imitated by a number of large manufacturing firms in this country. Mass production, coupled with standardisation, is chiefly responsible for the tremendous increase of productivity in this industry. The table on p. 16 of this book showed that, in the United States, the

[1] *The Social Aspects of Rationalisation*, p. 60.
[2] Urwick, L., *The Meaning of Rationalisation*, p. 119.

output of motor-cars per man-hour increased eightfold between 1909 and 1927, and no doubt the rise is still continuing.

A striking example of mass production combined with standardisation is afforded by an American manufacturer of motor-car parts. " He supplied a score or more of automobile factories. Each one bought from 10,000 to 500,000 parts a year, but each wanted some minor variation in the pattern. The constant change in machine set-up necessitated by these varying demands kept the manufacturer's plant in confusion. . . . Careful figuring showed him that he could cut his price in half, improve his delivery service, and yet make more money for himself, if he could induce all his customers to accept the same pattern. He laid the facts before them. They accepted the proposal."[1]

It is maintained by Filene,[2] a business man who made a fortune by the management of a large department store in Boston, U.S.A., that mass production does not simply imply large-scale production. " It is large-scale production based upon a clear understanding that increased production demands increased buying, and that the greatest total profits can be obtained only if the masses can and do enjoy a higher and ever higher standard of living. . . . Mass production, therefore, is *production for the masses.*" It is pointed out that Henry Ford gave higher wages than even the unions demanded, along with shorter hours, and he simultaneously reduced the price of his cars to a point which enabled the masses to buy them. On the other hand, it must be remembered that under mass production methods the worker has no control over the pace at which he works. This depends on the rate at which the machine is run, and if he is unable to main-

---

[1] Nat. Indust. Conference Board, *Industrial Standardisation*, New York, 1929.
[2] Filene, E. A., *Successful Living in this Machine Age*, London, 1932.

tain it he is replaced by someone else who can. The modern worker needs less skill and less training than his predecessor, but more slickness and amenability to monotonous drill.

Mass production can be greatly stimulated by additional incentives, such as those adopted by Bata in his shoe factory at Zlin, Czechoslovakia.[1] He instituted competition between the individual workshops by allowing the employees to participate both in profits and losses. The participation was collective, the profit and loss being reckoned for each single workshop and department. The allowance earned was in addition to the group piece rate paid. Competition between workshops and departments was carried so far that each of them seemed to operate as an independent undertaking. The supervisory staff were given an incentive to increase the efficiency of their departments, and other processes of rationalisation were adopted such as a planning department, flow work, organised elimination of waste and the abolition of middlemen between the purchase of raw material and distribution to the consumer.

INDUSTRIAL COMBINATIONS

Combinations between groups of employers have, in the past, been apt to increase the price of the articles manufactured rather than to reduce them, as they took the form of monopolies which aimed at controlling the entire output and eliminating free competition. Since the war combines have been created more especially in order to stabilise industry, and fusion or amalgamation has developed especially in the chemical industry, in iron and steel production, and in tobacco and cigarette manufacture. The big undertakings often swallow up a large number of small businesses, but they undoubtedly make for an

[1] *Bull. Internat. Management*, Aug. 1932, p. 125.

RATIONALISATION

increase of efficiency. The vertical trusts formed in this country after the war have not been altogether a success, and there is now a tendency towards horizontal trusts. Such trusts have, as their characteristics, (1) the centralisation of administrative, financial and technical control; (2) the concentration of production in the most modern units, and the steady elimination of subsidiary enterprises in favour of specialisation; (3) close association between finance and production in the execution of contracts and purchase of raw materials.[1]

Industrial combinations were adopted very freely in Germany as part of an organised plan of reconstruction in basic industries after the inflation period and the French occupation. The industrialists and technicians endeavoured to build up industries as a whole, whether organised as trusts or on a co-operative basis, in order to replace the kind of competition which leads to destructive price-cutting by mutual agreement on a common production and sales policy.[2] Technical and scientific knowledge and the fruits of research are pooled, and the immediate advantages for particular undertakings are subordinated to the general interest. Output, instead of being restricted in order to maintain high prices, is regulated with sufficient elasticity to meet fluctuations of demand without delay, so that price levels may be kept stable. Low production costs are aimed at and short-time working is reduced by concentrating production in the most efficient works. This programme of reconstruction was first carried out in the heavy industries, especially coal-mining and iron and steel production, but it has since been adapted to many other industries, including transport, agriculture, and trade, both wholesale and retail.

As an instance of industrial combination in Germany the

[1] Quigley, H., *Towards Industrial Recovery*, 1927.
[2] Meakin, W., *The Industrial Revolution*, pp. 16 *et seq.*

D

United Steel Trust may be mentioned. Production was concentrated in four factories instead of 14 or 16, and the remainder were closed. Specialisation was carried out wherever it was possible to concentrate the products of the rolling mills in the existing factories. Rails were produced only in two factories instead of the original eleven, and the same concentration was effected for section irons, tubes, etc. By installing trains of rolls the mills were able to manufacture everything from the raw material to the finished products. Again, in the German potash industry the number of mines actively worked has been reduced from 155 in 1921 to 93 in 1924 and 60 in 1927. The average output per factory rose 350 per cent. between 1921 and 1928, and the output per mine-worker rose from 1·56 tons in 1913 to 1·79 tons in 1924 and 3·08 tons in 1928. In the potash factories the output per worker per day rose from 3·33 metric tons in 1924 to 7·5 tons in 1928.[1]

The first stages of rationalisation in Germany led to a large displacement of surplus workers, but the subsequent general recovery had the effect—at any rate for a time—of reducing the total volume of unemployment almost to its pre-war level.

DISTRIBUTION

The disposal of the goods manufactured includes the processes of selling and advertising. Scientific management should be applied to the problem of marketing or " merchanting " in the same way as to workshop practice, for it similarly includes preparation, planning and policy, followed by execution. The planning or staff side of the selling organisation deals with the approach to the customers, the handling of the orders obtained, the allocation of stocks of finished goods, and the provision of

[1] *The Social Aspects of Rationalisation*, pp. 68 to 70.

a service of advice, information and inspection. Promises of delivery at certain dates are scrupulously carried out as they are based on organisation and plans which enable an exact forecast to be made of what can be achieved, while the older methods of promising delivery were based on general hopes and expectations which frequently could not be carried out. Scientific management is " management beforehand," and decides what *shall* happen, based as it is on knowledge of what can be done.[1]

The staff side of the selling department determines the detailed design and qualities of the products wanted, the geographical fields for their distribution, and the volume of demand at various price levels. It decides on methods of stimulating demand such as publicity policy and the instruction of salesmen and foreign agents in selling information.

In the transport of goods electric and gravity conveyers are commonly used in addition to trucks, in order to convey the goods from the place of production to the warehouse. From the warehouse they are delivered by motor-lorry to the railway station, or they may be loaded direct into railway wagons at private sidings in the factory. Frequently they are delivered straight from the factory over wide areas by means of a fleet of motor-vans.

TECHNOCRACY

Technocracy is a term adopted by a group of American engineers and scientists which connotes the methods and processes of rationalisation in combination with what they consider to be the best ways of dealing with the concomitant conditions of unemployment in the midst of plenty. The initiator of the movement, Mr. Howard Scott, is the chief engineer and technician of the Muscle Shoals project, and in company with a research staff of

[1] Pitman's *Dictionary of Industrial Administration*, p. 763.

engineers and a number of physicists, biochemists, and other scientists he established a research organisation for the purpose of making an " Energy Survey of North America."[1] The staff is engaged in analysing the physical resources of the country and their development during the last hundred years, and has plotted charts indicating the employment afforded, the production achieved and the energy expended in relation to hundreds of representative products. The results obtained are held to indicate that the technological advance made in industrial processes is so tremendous, especially during the last 25 years, that the existing social and economic structure is obsolete. Under the present economic system purchasing power is closely linked with the volume of employment, and as industry can only prosper when there is an adequate demand for its products at prices which make production profitable, it follows that production and trade are steadily decreasing while human want and misery are increasing. Technocracy asserts that the solution of the problem is to abandon the present price system, and adopt an entirely new system of distribution based on " energy certificates." It is maintained that energy is the real measure of human labour and human wealth, and its adoption should bring a proper synchronisation between production and consumption, so that all human needs are fully met and the necessary amount of human work equitably divided.

Details of the ways in which the new system is to be introduced do not seem to have been divulged, and the generalities hitherto vouchsafed afford us no sort of indication. It is stated[2] that " the unit income of the individual would be determined by . . . the time it takes for a complete cycle of the operating and production procedures to be completed. . . . Any unit of measure-

---

[1] *The Times*, Jan. 5th, 1933.
[2] Arkwright, F., *The A.B.C. of Technocracy*, London, 1933, p. 93; cf. Raymond, A., *What is Technocracy?* New York and London, 1933.

ment under technological control would be a certification of available energy converted. . . . This method of producing physical wealth and measuring its operation precludes the possibility of creating any kind of debt. It also eliminates the entire domain of philanthropy."

It is evident that any scheme for abating the conditions of unemployment and human want in the midst of plenty which are now associated with rationalisation must start on the basis of the price system at present in operation, and effect a transformation by gradual stages. One of the most important of these stages is undoubtedly the substantial reduction in the average hours of work, coupled with the payment of full wages. Doubtless it will be found in course of time that other changes are needed in addition, but it is not proposed to discuss them in the present book.

THE CHANGES OF EMPLOYMENT ASSOCIATED WITH RATIONALISATION

The Displacement of Labour.—We saw that the Geneva Economic Conference held in 1927 was alive to the fact that rationalisation might involve unemployment in its early stages, and several instances have been recorded in the previous section which showed a very marked displacement of labour. A few more instances may here be quoted.[1] (1) Rationalisation in Germany enabled gasworks to reduce their staff by a third or even a half, without affecting output. (2) A rubber factory was able to maintain its output although it reduced the number of its employees from 14,000 to 10,000, and a margarine factory achieved the same end with 1,000 workers instead of 1,600. (3) A slaughterhouse equipped on the American pattern now employs 22 slaughterers and 15 assistants to kill and dress 1,000 pigs in eight hours, whereas 150

[1] *Cf. The Social Aspects of Rationalisation*, pp. 246, 247, 251.

slaughterers were formerly required to do the same work in the same time. (4) Before the war a factory in Saxony employed 46 workers to make 4,000 mousetraps a day. Under the new system, 15 girls turn out 10,000 a day. (5) In Czechoslovakia the present production of window glass by Fourcault machines, in contrast to the hand labour employed in 1920, has increased production 100 per cent., though the number of workers employed has decreased 60 per cent. In the glass bottle industry, output has increased 43 per cent., while the number of workers employed has declined 60 per cent.

A number of manufacturing industries in the United States have been combined by the Federal Reserve Board,[1] and were found to yield the index numbers shown in the table:

Year.	Manufactured products.	Workers employed in factories.	Output per worker.	Wages paid per worker.
1919	100	100	100	100
1920	104	101	103	119
1921	80	77	104	103
1922	104	84	124	99
1923	120	97	124	108
1924	112	90	124	109
1925	125	93	134	111
1926	129	94	137	113
1927	126	92	137	113
1928	132	91	145	114
1929	142	94	151	117

It will be seen that between 1919 and 1929 the number of workers employed fell about 7 per cent., in spite of the fact that the total population of the United States increased about 16 per cent. Nevertheless, output rose 42 per cent., and this meant that the output per worker increased 51 per cent.

[1] *L.c.* p. 253.

It will be noted that the relationship between output and the number of workers employed was not steady. Evidently, therefore, other factors besides rationalisation were involved. This lack of relationship was also shown by some of the data recorded in Chapter I. We saw from the table on page 5 that the percentage of unemployed in almost all countries remained fairly steady between 1925 and 1929, and then increased rapidly; but the table on page 16 shows that productivity (in the U.S.A.) increased in individual industries at a very irregular rate.

For several reasons the unemployment caused by rationalisation is generally much less than the above quoted data suggest. The introduction of new machinery into an industry generally occurs gradually, and the construction of this machinery may entail the employment of a number of persons who would not otherwise get work. Again, the new machinery usually means a reduction of selling price. This may increase demand, and in consequence lead to increased production and re-employment. The reduction of selling prices also enables people to buy articles which they had been unable to afford previously, and thereby stimulates the demand for labour in other industries.

The Substitution of Labour.—The reduction of the workers employed in one industry is often accompanied by a more than corresponding increase of employment in other industries, though unfortunately the displaced workers are usually unsuited to the fresh vacancies arising. For instance, a report of the United States Bureau of Foreign and Domestic Commerce states[1] that, between 1920 and 1928, the factories decreased their employees by more than 900,000, largely owing to rationalisation; but the higher wages earned and the rise in the general standard of living so greatly increased the demand for motor-cars and other manufactured products that 1,280,000 more men found employment in driving and

[1] *Bull. Internat. Management Inst.*, Jan., 1929.

repairing the cars, 100,000 more men were required to attend to refrigerators, heaters, and other household appliances, 100,000 more life insurance agents were needed and, as a consequence of the greater desire for education, 185,000 more teachers obtained work. Another authority[1] states that, as the result of technological improvements in the United States between 1920 and 1927, 1,485,000 persons were displaced from agricultural and manufacturing occupations, but 1,300,000 persons obtained new jobs in the motoring industry, 407,000 in the medical and allied professions, and 616,000 in hotels, banks, insurance firms and the cinema industry. A third authority[2] states that while the output per wage-earner increased 40 per cent. between 1914 and 1925, manufacture and production increased 65 per cent., and this rise necessitated an increase of 1,500,000 wage-earners.

Change of employment often leads to the substitution of unskilled workers for the skilled and semi-skilled. An instance of this is afforded by comparative data of the various categories of workers at a chain-making factory (in England) in the years 1913 and 1927.[3] It will be seen from the table that during these years the

Year.	Men.					Women.
	Total men.	Fully-skilled craftsmen.	Semi-skilled machinists.	Unskilled.	Clerical.	
1913	1000	250	350	300	100	310
1927	680	250	185	85	160	680

number of men employed fell off 32 per cent., while the women, who were unskilled, more than doubled their

[1] Urwick, L., quoted from *The Social Aspects of Rationalisation*, p. 255.
[2] *L.c.* p. 259.
[3] *L.c.* p. 238.

number. It is true that the number of fully-skilled craftsmen was unchanged, but that of the semi-skilled male machinists was halved.

More striking evidence comes from the motor-car industry.[1] It was found that in a period of eleven years (1912 to 1923) the percentage of skilled workers employed at a modern factory (in the U.S.A.) was more than halved. The common labourers also fell off greatly, while the machine tenders and assemblers correspondingly increased in number.

In industrial disputes the skilled and the unskilled workers are sometimes on opposite sides. The skilled craftsman seeks to maintain his preferential wages and conditions, and is fearful of unemployment owing to his replacement by those below him in status. The less-skilled worker, on the other hand, is apt to resent the attitude of superiority of the craftsman and his exclusion from many jobs he could do equally well, so he may be disposed to back up the employer's efforts to break down the craft monopolies.[2]

The large-scale movements occurring in the industrial population of Great Britain are shown by the changes in the numbers of workers insured against unemployment.[3] The table on page 42 indicates the percentage changes in the numbers between 1923 and 1932, and it will be seen that while, in the building industry and the transport services the number of employees increased over 40 per cent., in the mining industry there was a reduction of 12 per cent. This was in spite of the fact that the total number of insured persons went up 15 per cent.

The next table[4] shows the annual changes in certain industries from 1923 onwards. It will be seen from this

---

[1] *L.c.* p. 262.
[2] Cole, G. D. H., *The Next Ten Years in British Social and Economic Policy*, London, 1929, p. 99.
[3] *Ministry of Labour Gazette*, Nov., 1932, p. 408.
[4] *L.c.* Nov. 1932, p. 430.

INSURED WORKERS (GREAT BRITAIN)

Group.	Estimated number insured in July, 1932.	Per cent. increase or decrease since July, 1923.
Building and contracting	1,147,280	+42·6
Transport, storage and distribution	2,824,300	+41·6
Miscellaneous	1,675,260	+27·7
Manufacturing	6,011,720	+ 5·3
Mining and quarrying	1,149,440	−12·0
All industries and services	12,808,000	+14·8

INSURED WORKERS (GREAT BRITAIN)

Industry.	Number of insured persons (16 to 64).	Index numbers.				
		1923.	1926.	1928.	1930.	1932.
Expanding industries :						
Electrical engineering	94,080	100	125·4	133·3	150·3	157·4
Distributive trades	1,950,240	100	120·8	131·0	143·4	158·5
Printing, bookbinding	284,770	100	109·9	114·0	122·4	128·0
Building	856,910	100	112·4	119·8	122·2	125·8
Tailoring	211,660	100	104·5	108·3	110·0	115·4
Contracting industries :						
Boots and shoes	137,970	100	102·4	97·4	98·3	99·9
Cotton	517,950	100	101·3	99·0	100·8	92·6
General engineering	551,200	100	91·8	90·7	92·3	85·9
Steel melting, rolling	167,760	100	91·2	87·6	88·7	82·3
Shipbuilding and repairing	181,930	100	82·6	77·7	78·6	69·8

table and from Fig. 5 that in certain industries there was a fairly steady rise of employment, while in others there was

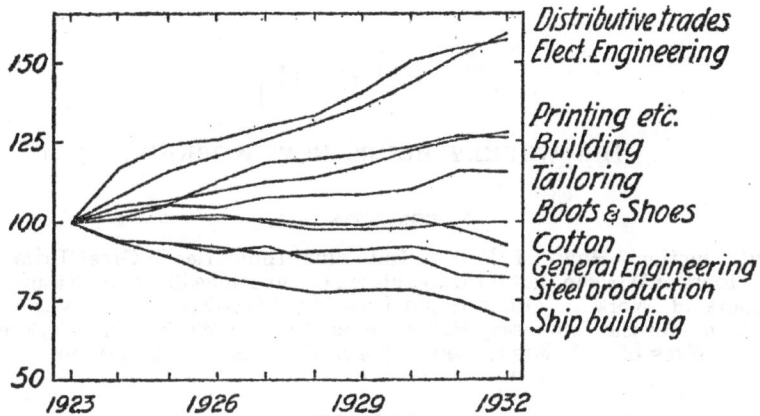

FIG. 5.—Changes in the number of insured persons (Great Britain).

a steady though less substantial fall. Only in the boot and shoe and the cotton industries did employment remain more or less stationary.

CHAPTER III

THE WEEKLY HOURS NOW WORKED

CONTENTS

Introduction—Hours of Work in Individual Industries in Great Britain—Hours of Work in Certain Unregulated Occupations in Great Britain—Hours of Work in Other Countries—The Five-Day Week—Various Schemes for the Temporary Reduction in Hours of Work—The Working Week of 40 Hours or Less—Overhead Costs—Shift Systems

INTRODUCTION

BEFORE the Great War a working week of 52 to $55\frac{1}{2}$ hours was customary in most industries, though a 48-hour week was gradually being introduced in some of them. Continuous processes, such as are met with in the iron and steel industry, were usually run by two 12-hour shifts, and some of the men averaged 84 hours per week, inclusive of meals. After the war, three 8-hour shifts were substituted in this industry, and a 47- or 48-hour week was introduced in the majority of the other industries. In consequence, the hours of work in industry as a whole were reduced about 10 per cent.

The total reductions of hours among insured persons are recorded every year in the *Ministry of Labour Gazette*,[1] and from the table on page 45 it will be seen that in 1919 over six million workers had their hours of labour reduced, the aggregate reduction amounting to over 40 million hours per week. There was a further substantial reduction in 1920, but from that time onwards up to the present day there has been no general trend towards a

---

[1] *Ministry of Labour Gazette*, Jan., 1934, p. 5.

THE WEEKLY HOURS NOW WORKED

further reduction of hours. In fact, it will be seen that an average for the years 1921–33 shows an *increase* of about 250,000 hours per week. This increase is due almost entirely to the coal-miners, who had their working

Year.	Number of workpeople whose hours of labour were		Aggregate net increase (+) or decrease (—) in weekly hours.
	Increased.	Reduced.	
1919	1,150	6,305,000	— 40,651,000
1920	2,000	570,000	— 2,114,000
1921	31,500	12,900	+ 14,500
1922	16,000	302,700	— 93,000
1923	325,000	9,600	+ 108,750
1924	13,150	16,150	+ 12,500
1925	1,300	3,925	— 11,750
1926	934,200	340	+ 3,985,000
1927	18,700	1,700	+ 59,000
1928	1,400	2,000	— 200
1929	4,050	1,050	+ 8,750
1930	13,175	349,225	— 873,500
1931	294,000	111,000	+ 142,000
1932	6,000	3,750	+ 7,000
1933	2,500	11,000	— 35,000
Mean per year (1921–33) ...	127,767	63,488	+ 255,696

shift increased from $7\frac{1}{2}$ to 8 hours after the prolonged mining dispute in 1926. In 1930 there was a reversion to the $7\frac{1}{2}$-hour shift in some districts and under certain conditions, but only a third of the miners were affected. The smaller changes of hours in 1922 and 1923 relate mostly to the building trades.

NORMAL HOURS OF WORK OF ADULT MALE WORKERS IN GREAT BRITAIN, OCTOBER, 1932

Industry and Occupation.	Birmingham.	Bristol.	Glasgow.	Leeds.	London.	Manchester.	Newcastle.
Mechanical engineering — Fitters, turners	47	47	47	47	47	47	47
Mechanical engineering — Iron-moulders	47	47	47	47	47	47	47
Building — Bricklayers, masons	47	47	47	47	47	47	47
Building — Carpenters, joiners	44–46·5	41·5–44	39–44	44–46·5	44	44–46·5	44
Building — Painters	44–46·5	41·5–44	41·5–44	44–46·5	44	44–46·5	44
Building — Plumbers	47	47	47	47	47	47	47
Furniture-making — Cabinet-makers	47	47	47	47	47	46·5	47
Furniture-making — Upholsterers	47	47	47	47	47	46·5	47
Printing and bookbinding — Hand compositors	48	48	48	48	48	48	48
Printing and bookbinding — Machine compositors	48	48	48	48	48	48	48
Printing and bookbinding — Bookbinders	48	48	48	48	48	48	48
Food industry — Bakers	48	48	45	48	48	48	48
Transport — Trams and buses (drivers, conductors)	48	48	48	48	48	48	48
Transport — Motor- and horse-drivers	48	48	48	48	48	48	48
Transport — Railway porters	48	48	48	48	48	48	48
Electric power — Fitters	47	47	48	47	47	47	47
Local authorities (unskilled labourers)	47	47	48	47	47	47	47

THE WEEKLY HOURS NOW WORKED

HOURS OF WORK IN INDIVIDUAL INDUSTRIES IN GREAT BRITAIN

The hours of work in a number of the industries pursued in Great Britain have recently been recorded in the *International Labour Review*.[1] They relate to the month of October, 1932, and we see that with very few exceptions they are either 47 or 48 hours per week in all the big towns where they were investigated. The exceptions mostly relate to the building and allied trades, in which the hours of work vary with the season. It will be seen from the next table[2] that they ranged from 44 to $49\frac{1}{2}$ hours in summer, and from $41\frac{1}{2}$ to $44\frac{1}{2}$ hours in winter.

Occupation.	Season.	London, Newcastle.	Leeds, Manchester, Birmingham.	Bristol.	Glasgow.
Bricklayers, masons, carpenters, joiners, plumbers, painters, labourers ...	summer	44	$46\frac{1}{2}$	44	44
	winter	44	44	$41\frac{1}{2}$	$41\frac{1}{2}$
Concrete-workers	summer	$49\frac{1}{2}$	$49\frac{1}{2}$	$49\frac{1}{2}$	—
	winter	$44\frac{1}{2}$	$44\frac{1}{2}$	$44\frac{1}{2}$	—

These nominal hours of work are subject to a good deal of variation at the hands of individual employers. The table on page 48 shows the result of a detailed enquiry, made in October, 1924,[3] covering over five million workpeople. It will be seen that about a seventh of them worked for 44 hours or less per week, a third worked 47 hours, rather over a third worked 48 hours, and a small proportion over

---

[1] *Internat. Labour Review*, 27, p. 815, 1933.
[2] *Internat. Labour Review*, 26, p. 97, 1932.
[3] *Ministry of Labour Gazette*, July, 1927, p. 251.

Industry Group.	Number of workpeople covered.	Percentage of workpeople whose normal weekly hours were:						Average weekly normal hours.
		44 or less.	44¾ to 46¾	47	47¼ to 47¾	48	Over 48.	
Pottery, Brick, Glass, Chemical, etc.	277,828	11·3	7·8	39·5	2·8	26·8	11·8	47·4
Metal	1,362,199	10·0	3·4	76·1	0·9	4·6	5·0	46·7
Textile...	1,031,821	3·6	1·8	2·2	0·5	89·0	2·9	47·9
Clothing	487,318	18·5	15·2	8·1	2·3	52·6	3·3	46·7
Food, drink, tobacco ...	398,911	15·5	8·8	19·2	2·7	39·8	14·0	47·5
Woodworking...	179,516	25·1	9·2	39·6	2·3	10·1	13·7	46·8
Paper, printing, etc. ...	238,004	11·0	5·0	2·8	2·3	75·3	3·6	47·3
Building, etc.	289,783	67·2	12·6	5·5	0·6	2·5	11·6	45·4
Other industries	306,164	14·2	8·0	19·5	1·9	41·1	15·3	47·3
Public utility services ...	466,366	7·6	3·2	48·1	0·4	28·1	12·6	47·6
Government industrial establishments	101,810	1·2	0·1	65·3	0·0	32·6	0·8	47·3
All the above	5,139,720	13·7	5·8	33·7	1·3	38·2	7·3	47·1

THE WEEKLY HOURS NOW WORKED

48 hours. Even this table does not represent the hours actually worked, for an enquiry made for a four-week period among firms employing over three million workpeople showed that they worked 1·3 hours less, on an average, than those recorded in the last column of the table.

In agriculture there is also a seasonal variation in the hours of work, and the next table shows that in 1931 there

INCREASE OF HOURS WORKED IN AGRICULTURE (1931).

County.	New hours.		Previous hours.		Increase.	
	Summer.	Winter.	Summer.	Winter.	Summer.	Winter.
Radnorshire and Brecknockshire	54	50	54	48	0	2
Worcestershire	52	48	50½	48	1½	0
Leicestershire	56½	54	54	54	2½	0
Rutland	56½	54	54	50	2½	4
Dorset	53½	48	51	48	2½	0
Hampshire and Isle of Wight	53½	48	51	48	2½	0
Nottinghamshire	52½	50	50	50	2½	0
Northamptonshire	54	50	50	48	4	2
Warwickshire	52	48	50	48	2	0
Norfolk	53	48	50	48	3	0
Mean	53·8	49·8	51·5	49	2·3	0·8

was an increase of about 2½ hours per week in the time worked in summer in most of the counties for which records are quoted. The hours now average nearly 54 in summer and 50 in winter, so they are substantially longer than those worked in manufacturing industries.

HOURS OF WORK IN CERTAIN UNREGULATED OCCUPATIONS IN GREAT BRITAIN

Young Persons.—The hours of work for women and young persons (aged 14 to 18) are limited to $55\frac{1}{2}$ a week in textile factories, exclusive of meals, and to 60 hours in other factories (exclusive of meals and overtime). In shops there is a permissible maximum of $65\frac{1}{2}$ hours, exclusive of meals, but there is still no regulation of hours for young persons (*a*) in offices and warehouses, (*b*) in domestic service, hotels and clubs, (*c*) in agriculture, and (*d*) as messenger boys, van boys, etc. An attempt to regularise these occupations was made by a Departmental Committee in 1913,[1] and it was recommended that the hours in certain occupations should be regulated by means of by-laws administered by the Local Authorities. A weekly limit of 70 hours inclusive of meal-times was suggested, meal-times to be not less than $1\frac{1}{2}$ hours a day; but no action was taken as the result of the recommendation.

The National Advisory Council for Juvenile Employment was asked by the Ministry of Labour in 1930 to make an enquiry into the employment of young persons in unregulated occupations, and they obtained information from over 127,000 boys and girls aged 14 to 18. The data[2] on page 51 represent their average hours of work, exclusive of meal-times.

It will be seen that nearly half the young persons worked over 48 hours per week, and a sixth of them over 54 hours. A majority of the Council, the representatives of the employers dissenting, considered that there is need for the further regulation of the hours of the boys and girls concerned.[3]

Catering Trade.—An enquiry made by the Ministry of

[1] *Britain's Industrial Future*, p. 387, London, 1928. [2] *Ministry of Labour Gazette*, Feb., 1932, p. 47.
[3] A Bill is now being passed through Parliament which reduces the normal working hours of young persons to 48 a week.

THE WEEKLY HOURS NOW WORKED

Labour[1] in the catering trade showed that (in November, 1929) a very long working week was frequently demanded from the men and women. It will be seen from the table on page 52 that in fair-sized hotels about 37 per cent. of the employees worked 60 hours or more, and 13 to 18 per cent. of them 66 hours or more, but conditions were better in public-houses, inns and restaurants.

	Number covered by inquiry.	Percentage whose normal weekly hours were:		
		Up to and including 48.	Over 48, and up to and including 54.	Over 54.
Errand boys	72,848	47·9	31·1	21·0
Errand girls	4,779	67·2	23·6	9·2
Van boys	12,692	54·4	28·0	17·6
Warehouse boys	12,420	85·2	12·0	2·8
Warehouse girls	6,957	85·0	14·4	0·6
Messenger boys	6,887	69·2	24·0	6·8
Messenger girls	1,681	73·6	25·4	1·0
Petrol-pump boys	1,951	49·8	26·0	24·2
Other occupations	7,177	59·7	26·7	13·6
Total	127,392	57·1	26·9	16·0

Baking.—In the baking industry (in London) the nominal 48-hour week is seldom kept, except in large factories. The baker has to continue his baking until the desired output is reached, and this may take 60, 70 or 80 hours. It is estimated that about one-third of the operative bakers work 70 to 80 hours a week, though it is stated that in factories the average week's work is 56 hours.[2]

Distributive Trades.—The number of persons engaged in wholesale and retail distribution in Great Britain is very

[1] *L.c.*, Sept., 1930, p. 320.
[2] *New Survey of London Life and Labour*, Vol. V, p. 46, 1933.

large. It is stated[1] to be three million in round numbers, of whom two million are employees and one million employers or one-man business persons, such as small shopkeepers. According to the census of 1921, 540,000 persons were then employed in distribution in Greater London alone. About a quarter of them were described as retail shop assistants, but their number has so greatly increased since 1921 that they now (in 1934) probably number about 240,000. Their weekly hours of work are said to vary

Adult workers.	Number of workers.	Percentage with weekly hours of					
		less than 48.	48.	over 48 under 54.	54 and under 60.	60 and under 66.	66 and over.
Males in hotels (over 10 bedrooms)	7,437	5·9	8·0	19·6	29·2	24·7	12·6
,, in public-houses and inns	1,941	49·3	4·4	9·7	13·3	18·6	4·7
,, in licensed restaurants	3,649	19·3	12·6	22·7	33·4	7·0	5·0
Women in hotels (over 10 bedrooms)	5,422	8·5	7·4	17·6	28·8	19·6	18·1
,, in public-houses and inns	1,828	56·1	3·6	9·7	14·4	13·1	0·3
,, in licensed restaurants	3,605	27·0	6·7	46·1	13·9	5·3	0·0

from 47 in departmental stores to 51 in draper's shops and 62 in sweet and chocolate shops ; but this estimate does not include overtime, which at certain rush periods may be very great.[2] The hours are probably longer than these in some districts, for an enquiry made among a sample of

[1] Hilton, J., "Industrial Britain." Synopsis of Talks, broadcast, Jan.-Mar., 1934.
[2] *New Survey of London Life and Labour*, Vol. V, p. 149, 1933.

Liverpool shop assistants,[1] 540 in number, showed that 35 per cent. of them worked 48 hours or less, 41 per cent. worked over 48 hours but under 56 hours, 9 per cent. worked over 56 hours and under 60, while 15 per cent. worked 60 or more hours. The bakers and confectioners appeared to be the most heavily worked, a fourth of them working 60 hours or more.

Cinema Trade.—The hours of work in this new and rapidly-growing industry are often scandalously long. The normal working day is 14 hours for men and 11 hours for women, including meal-times.[2] Allowing for these, the hours of actual work are $66\frac{1}{3}$ for men and $52\frac{1}{3}$ for women, and the day's work is not over till 11 p.m., or even later. Overtime is frequently worked but rarely paid for, and as the trade is practically unorganised, union action is impossible.

THE HOURS OF WORK IN OTHER COUNTRIES

The normal hours of work in other countries are, for the most part, similar to those met with in Great Britain. The table[3] on page 54 records the hours worked in 1932 in a number of typical industries in groups of large towns situated in Europe, the United States, and Australia. It will be seen that, with a few exceptions, a 48-hour week is worked in every country except the United States, Poland and Belgrade (Yugoslavia). The hours in the United States ranged from 40 to 56·5, and, as is subsequently mentioned, they now range from 30 hours upwards. In Poland a uniform 46-hour week is worked, but in Belgrade the hours run from 48 to 73.

The coal-mining industry has to be considered apart

[1] Report on "New Aspects of the Problem of Hours of Work," Internat. Assn. for Social Progress, London, 1933.
[2] *L.c.* p. 40.
[3] *Internat. Lab. Rev.*, 26, p. 97, 1932.

NORMAL HOURS OF LABOUR IN CERTAIN LARGE TOWNS

	France, 4 towns.	Germany, 6 towns.	Italy, 6 towns.	Spain, 4 towns.	Poland, 4 towns.	Netherlands, 4 towns.	Belgium, Brussels.	Sweden, 3 towns.	Denmark, Copenhagen.	Austria, 3 towns.	Yugoslavia, Belgrade.	Yugoslavia, Zagreb.	U.S.A. 10 towns.	Australia, 2 towns.
Mechanical engineering	48	48	48	48	46	48	48	48	48	48	60	48	42·9	44
Building ...	48	44-48	48	48	46	48	48	48	48	48	66	48	56·5	44
Furniture-making	48	48	48	48	46	48	48	48	48	48	60	48	40-48	48
Printing and bookbinding	48	48	48	48	46	48	48	48	48	48	48	48	46·4–	44
Food industry (baking)	48	48	48	48	46	48	48	48	48	48	73	48	53·4	44
Transport {Trams, buses	48	44-51	48	48	46	48	—	50	—	—	48	48-54	44-48	44-48
Cartage	48	48	48	48	46	48-62½	—	48	49-57	48	48	48-50	48	48
Railways ...	48	50·4	48	48	46	48	—	48	—	—	60	48-54	—	—
Electric power distribution	48	48	48	48	46	48	48	48	48	48	60	48	40-48	—
Local authorities (labourers)	48	48	48	48	46	48	—	48	48	—	—	50	—	44-48

THE WEEKLY HOURS NOW WORKED

from other industries, as the comparison of the data obtained from different countries is rather uncertain. In order to calculate the actual time spent underground, it is usual to add *one* winding time to the nominal length of shift. The winding of the whole of the underground men usually takes half an hour down and half an hour up, so the men spend an average time of half an hour over the two windings. The accompanying table, taken from the

Country.	Time spent in mine by underground workers.				Surface workers.			
	Shift.		Week.		Shift.		Week.	
	h.	m.	h.	m.	h.	m.	h.	m.
Belgium	8	0	48	0	8	0	48	0
Czechoslovakia	7	28	44	48	7	45	46	30
France	7	52	47	12	8	0	48	0
Great Britain (average) ...	8	0	43	50	7 to 8	20 15	44 to 49	0 30
Netherlands	8	10	47	0	—	—	—	—
Poland (Upper Silesia) ...	8	2	48	12	8	0	48	0
Poland (Dombrowa and Cracow)	8	30	49	0	8	0	46	0
Saar	7	30			7 to 8	30 0		

Ministry of Labour Gazette,[1] shows the times spent underground and on the surface in 1931. In some countries the duration of the shift worked on Saturdays is less than on other week-days, so the weekly hours of work may be shorter than in other countries, though the ordinary shift is longer.

[1] *Ministry of Labour Gazette*, Oct., 1933, p. 364.

THE FIVE-DAY WEEK

A system of work which often includes a reduction in the total weekly hours of labour is the five-day week. The ordinary working week extends over six full days in most countries, but in Great Britain no work is done on Saturday afternoons in any except a few continuous industries (*e.g.*, iron smelting in blast furnaces), so the normal working week is $5\frac{1}{2}$ days. Of recent years a movement in favour of the abolition of the half-day's work on Saturday has been rapidly gaining ground in this country and America. The system has certain manifest advantages both to the workers and to the employers. The men are able to utilise their free Saturday in getting open-air exercise, either by working at their allotments and gardens, or by playing games. Alternatively, they may do odd jobs about the home, or indulge in other forms of indoor amusement and relaxation. The women usually do shopping and housework, and they may work so hard at these pursuits that the free day is no holiday at all. Again, the workers are saved the expense of travelling from their homes to the factory in order to do a rather broken and unsatisfactory half-day of work. The management, for their part, are able to save substantial overhead costs for heating the factory and raising steam, while they get better opportunities for repairing machinery and overhauling the plant. In consequence, stoppages of production owing to mechanical breakdowns may be considerably reduced. Again, the employers have found that in many cases absenteeism from sickness is reduced, and time-keeping improves.

The factory inspectors in this country have paid special attention to the growth of the five-day week system, and the annual reports of the Chief Inspector make frequent references to it. They are almost uniformly favourable.

For instance, it is reported[1] that " the workers, and indeed the managers, seem to be almost unanimously in favour of it. . . . It is quite usual for the managers to say that young workers seem much fresher when they have had the longer week-end holiday." Again, we read[2] that a large motor-car works finds that with two years' experience " the five-day week is an unqualified success from both the firm's and the workers' point of view. Establishment expenses have been reduced, and it is found that the men, if overtime has to be worked, prefer to come in on Saturday morning rather than work in the week-day evenings."

One firm took a ballot among their employees, after the five-day week had been in operation for seven years in the works and for fifteen months in the office.[3] As a result, 208 workers said that they preferred to retain the present system, and only 4 wished to revert to the $5\frac{1}{2}$-day week. Only 15 out of the 212 workers considered that the system had any disadvantages, and when questioned about the effect of the system on health, 96 workers said that it had a good effect, 89 that it had no effect, and 4 that it had a bad one. The extra rest and change was found to be beneficial, and the long week-end refreshing.

The objections to the system mostly concerned the long day's work. As the working week was $47\frac{1}{2}$ hours, this meant $9\frac{1}{2}$ hours a day. Apparently two $4\frac{3}{4}$-hour spells were worked, and a 10-minute rest pause was given during each of them. This was said by some workers to be essential, and it certainly is important where women are concerned. The brief pause is advantageous for physiological reasons, especially in the morning spell of work, for it enables the workers to take a little food during the period of six hours which often elapses between breakfast and dinner. It is also important for psychological

---

[1] Annual Report of Chief Inspector of Factories for 1925, p. 44.
[2] *Industrial Welfare*, 1929, p. 53.
[3] *L.c.*, 1933, June, p. xix.

reasons, dependent chiefly on relief from monotony.[1] An investigation in a number of factories where women were engaged on various repetition processes showed that the introduction of a rest pause of 7 to 10 minutes' duration in the morning work spell (which lasted $4\frac{1}{2}$ or $4\frac{3}{4}$ hours) led to an improvement of 6 per cent. in the output, in spite of the loss of working time.[2]

The 1930 Report of the Chief Inspector of Factories states that the five-day week system had been adopted in 744 works, which between them employed over 83,000 workpeople. A sixth of these workers were employed in the furniture trade and another sixth in the metal trades, while the clothing trade accounted for 9,300 of them. The hours worked were generally 47 or 48, but in a quarter of the factories the hours were about 45 per week. Only in 4 per cent. of them were they less than 45 hours, but in one factory (for match manufacture) the hours were reduced to 40 a week. The piecework production was said to be practically as great as in the previous 47-hour regime, while in a furniture factory the output during the 45-hour week was said to be as great as during the previous 54-hour week.

Other objections to the system are that the long day's work may make the free time in the evenings very short, and prevent attendance at evening classes. In some factories (on a 48-hour week) the hours of work are 6 to 8 a.m., 8.30 to 12.30 p.m., and 1.30 to 5.30 p.m. on Tuesday to Friday, with a shorter working day on Monday. The very early start is unpleasant on dark winter mornings, and if a 45-hour week is worked instead of one of 48 hours, it can easily be avoided. If work begins at 7.30 or 8 a.m. two $4\frac{1}{2}$-hour spells are usually arranged for, and work ends at 5.30 or 6 p.m. If a 40-hour week is adopted two 4-hour

[1] Vernon, H. M., Vernon, M. D., and Lorrain-Smith, I., Report No. 47 of Indust. Fatigue Research Board, 1928.
[2] Vernon, H. M., Bedford, T., and Warner, C. G., Report No. 25 of Indust. Fatigue Research Board, 1924.

spells, running from 8 a.m. to 12 noon, and from 1 to 5 p.m., would usually be worked. This is an admirable arrangement of working hours, for the 4-hour spells are not so long as to require the interposition of a rest pause, such as is desirable with $4\frac{1}{2}$- to 5-hour spells. Also it is found that in many industrial occupations the rate of production is distinctly higher on an 8-hour day than on a 9-hour day, owing to the diminution of fatigue. This question of output in relation to hours of work is discussed in a subsequent chapter.

In America the five-day week system has made as rapid progress as in this country. In 1926 Henry Ford adopted a five-day week at his motor-car factories at Detroit, and 250,000 workers had their hours of work reduced to 40 per week. Ford favoured the system, not on humanitarian grounds, but because the extra leisure afforded by the free day enabled the working men to cultivate a higher standard of living, and they consequently tended to increase their purchases (*e.g.*, of motor-cars). An enquiry made by the National Industrial Conference Board[1] resulted in information respecting 270 establishments, employing in aggregate 216,921 workers on the five-day system. This total, which was ascertained in 1928, does not represent nearly all the workers under the system, for it was stated at the Annual Congress of the American Federation of Labour in 1930 that 532,894 workers were on the five-day week.[2]

The Industrial Conference Board was able to obtain information concerning output and hours of work in 219 establishments, and of these 3 had slightly increased their hours of work, 27 had kept them unchanged, and 189 had reduced them. The reduction was usually substantial, and 104 of the establishments had adopted a 40-hour

---

[1] National Industrial Conference Board, *The Five-Day Week in Manufacturing Industries*, New York, 1929.
[2] *The Social Aspects of Rationalisation*, p. 156, 1931.

week. Output data were supplied by 127 companies, of which 94 had reduced hours of work. The effect of this reduction was to increase output in 18 of the companies, to cause no change in 46 of them, to cause a loss proportional to the reduction of hours in 24 of them, and to cause a more substantial loss in 6. Hence nearly 70 per cent. of all the establishments suffered no loss of output, but the information provided is not very trustworthy, as the conditions of production were changed in some instances.

The five-day week does not seem to have made much progress in most other countries, but in Czechoslovakia it is being taken up on a substantial scale. The Bata Shoe Company at Zlin established a five-day week of 45 hours in 1930, and output was found to remain as high as under the previous 48-hour system. Altogether 17,000 workers in the industry, or 60 per cent. of the whole number, have come on to the five-day week, and several factories in other industries have adopted it.[1]

VARIOUS SCHEMES FOR THE TEMPORARY REDUCTION OF HOURS OF WORK

During the present period of economic depression, a number of temporary schemes of reduction in the hours of labour have been adopted in order to spread the available work over a larger number of persons, and so reduce the number of discharges or avoid them altogether. Doubtless many of these schemes will be abandoned when trade revives, but they are exceedingly valuable as a temporary measure, and have kept in employment many hundreds of thousands of persons who would otherwise be workless. Usually the number of workplaces in a factory, mine, or yard, is limited to a certain figure,

[1] *L.c.* p. 153.

THE WEEKLY HOURS NOW WORKED

so the number of workers employed at one and the same time cannot be increased. It may, therefore, be impossible to substitute, *e.g.*, a 6-hour or a 7-hour day for the usual 8- or 9-hour day, and employ a proportionately larger number of workers. The same objection applies to the substitution of a 5- or a 4-day week for the usual one of $5\frac{1}{2}$ or 6 days.

A method of employment which avoids the difficulty of limited workplaces is that of *rotation*. If, in a workshop which normally employs 5 men on a certain class of work for 6 days a week, each man is required to take one day off, it will be possible to employ an additional man. Alternatively, each of the 6 men may be laid off from work for one week in six. This system of laying off can sometimes be extended to groups of workers, the staff of an undertaking or a department being increased by one-fifth, and divided into six groups. Each group works for five weeks, and is laid off for one week. For instance, a rotation agreement relating to 9,000 employees at restaurants and hotels in the province of Milan was made for the period October, 1932, to March, 1933. According to the agreement the waiters alternate on a system of weekly rotation with those at present out of work, while the employees at restaurants are given a special holiday of twelve days without pay.[1]

The rotation system may cover months instead of weeks, as in the Krümper system,[2] which has been widely adopted in certain districts in Germany. Under this system a specified proportion of the staff, ranging from a quarter to a tenth, is suspended in rotation for a period of a week or a month. While the workers are laid off they receive unemployment benefit at a reduced rate. For instance, a collective agreement was concluded in October, 1931, in the Lower Silesian coalfield, under which the

[1] *Hours of Work and Unemployment*, p. 94.
[2] *L.c.* p. 85.

number of workers was increased by a sixth, and a seventh of the total number were laid off each month in rotation. By this measure it was possible to avoid the discharge of 1,800 workers. As a concrete instance of rotation in this country, the scheme adopted at the Blaenavon Collieries may be mentioned.[1] The company to whom the pits belong found that there was sufficient work for only 1,200 men, while 850 were left idle. The men themselves, on their own initiative, decided to share the work and the pay and the unemployment coupled with the unemployment benefit, so as to prevent the enforced idleness of their fellows. The South Wales Miners' Federation has approved the scheme, and it is to be hoped that it will be imitated in other parts of the coalfield.

When the available work is so much reduced that there is no difficulty about providing sufficient workplaces, the simplest plan for keeping the maximum number of persons employed is to cut down the hours for which the plant is run each day, or the number of working days in the week. For instance, a large German firm producing electrical apparatus reduced the working day in its establishments to six hours, and consequently was able to employ a larger staff in 1931 than in 1930, in spite of the depression.[2]

The most usual plan is to arrange hours and days so as to yield a 40-hour week of work. For instance, two municipalities in Czechoslovakia introduced a 40-hour week in their services and undertakings, and at Bratislava it was possible, by this means, to re-employ 16 per cent. of those out of work. In Germany, a similar reduction of hours in Berlin, Hamburg, and other large towns (in December, 1930) has not only prevented the discharge of large numbers of workers, but has even led to the engage-

---

[1] *The Times*, Nov. 21st, 1933.
[2] *Hours of Work and Unemployment*, p. 91.

ment of some thousands of the unemployed.[1] In Belgium the provincial councils of Antwerp and East Flanders in 1931 introduced a clause imposing a 40-hour week in the contracts for public works, and in New South Wales public contracts likewise stipulate that the hours may not exceed 40 per week. A wage rate calculated on a 44-hour basis is maintained in this latter instance, but in the majority of the other instances recorded wages appear to have been reduced in proportion to the reduced hours. In Germany the Federal Government (in September, 1931) were given power to reduce the hours of work in certain branches of industry and public offices to 40 a week, the employers being expressly authorised to reduce wages by an amount corresponding to the reduction of hours.[2]

In industries run continuously the usual custom is to work three 8-hour shifts, so the number of men employed can be increased by a third if four 6-hour shifts are substituted. For instance, the Kellogg Food Company (U.S.A.) adopted this plan in December, 1930, and when doing so they increased the hourly rate of pay $12\frac{1}{2}$ per cent. Some large oil factories in Germany adopted a similar plan in October, 1930, and were thereby enabled to engage 350 workers in addition to the 1,000 already employed, but no wage compensation was granted.[3] The German sheet-glass industry introduced the four-shift system in August, 1932, and the Czechoslovakian glass factories have followed suit. One of the principal glass factories in the United States has adopted it, and has thereby been enabled to engage 2,000 additional workers.

In the United States various schemes for spreading the available work over as many persons as possible have been adopted on a very large scale. In March, 1932, the President's Organisation for Unemployment Relief endeavoured

[1] *L.c.* p. 70.
[2] *L.c.* p. 73.
[3] *L.c.* pp. 79, 80, 84, 85.

to ascertain the extent to which the various methods were adopted,[1] and out of 4,926 undertakings which gave information it appeared that :

> 3,857 undertakings had reduced the number of days per week.
> 2,336 undertakings had reduced the number of hours per day.
> 380 undertakings had adopted shorter shifts in their continuous work.
> 1,338 undertakings had adopted alternating shifts or individuals.
> 1,170 undertakings had adopted a system of rotation of days off.

It will be noted that the total number of cases is much larger than the number of undertakings supplying information. This was because many of them made use of several of the methods of reducing hours.

THE WORKING WEEK OF FORTY HOURS OR LESS

We have seen that most of the firms and organisations adopting the temporary schemes of employment above described were so hard hit by the economic depression that they had to reduce wages in proportion to the reduction of hours. A few of them paid a somewhat higher rate, but scarcely any paid the same wages as were previously paid for the normal working week. For some years past the workers' organisations have been advocating the *permanent* adoption of a 40-hour week, without reduction of wages, and in April, 1932, the 16th Session of the International Labour Conference adopted a resolution inviting the International Labour Office " to investigate the question of the legal institution of the forty-hour week

---

[1] *Monthly Labour Review*, Sept., 1932, p. 489.

in all industrial countries, with a view to the early adoption of international regulations on the subject."[1] A resolution was also brought forward that the 40-hour week should not involve any reduction of wages, but it obtained only 21 votes, there being 32 adverse votes and 17 abstentions. Representatives of the employers said that the proposed reform involved insuperable practical and technical difficulties, and economic difficulties which it would be impossible to overcome. Some employers said that the 40-hour week would raise the cost of production 15 or even 20 per cent. and would tend to upset the market still further than at present.

In the following year (January 10th-25th, 1933) a Tripartite Preparatory Conference on reduction of hours of work was held at Geneva,[2] and a number of questions were discussed and voted upon. A resolution was adopted to the effect that a Convention should be aimed at by an International Labour Conference, to be held at a subsequent date. Of the Government delegates present 18 voted in favour of this resolution and 3 against; of the employers' representatives, 0 in favour and 18 against, and of the workers' representatives, 18 in favour and 0 against. A resolution to the effect that the Convention should provide that the average working week was not to exceed 40 hours, subject to such exceptions as the Convention may provide, was adopted by 35 votes to 2, but the employers' group abstained from voting as they said that they were not prepared to take any responsibility in drawing up a Convention. They further stated that " We pointed out clearly to the Conference that nothing had taken place which led us to change our attitude of complete opposition to the proposals submitted to the Conference." The workers' group, in reply, said that

[1] Maurette, F., " The Preparatory Conference on the Forty-Hour Week," *Internat. Lab. Rev.*, 27, p. 299, 1933.
[2] Report of the Tripartite Preparatory Conference, Report V. Internat. Lab. Conf., Geneva, 1933.

"Whereas the number of unemployed throughout the world is at least 30 millions, we note that since the Conference decided that it was desirable to aim at a Convention concerning the reduction of hours of work as a remedy for unemployment, the employers' group has taken up a purely negative attitude. . . . The workers' group . . . finds that the idea of the reduction of hours of work and the maintenance of the standard of living of the workers as a remedy for unemployment has been accepted by a majority which includes the governments of the chief industrial countries of Europe with one single exception."

The International Labour Conference debated the proposal for a universal 40-hour week in June, 1933, and it was opposed by the representatives of the employers (except the Italians), and by several Government representatives. However, the Swedish representative was in favour of the "second reading" of the 40-hour week proposal, and he stated that more than 25 per cent. of Swedish industry was already working 40 hours or less a week.[1] A representative of the workers said that it might eventually need even a 30-hour week to solve the unemployment problem.

It has been calculated[2] that the establishment of a 40-hour week in the cotton industry in Great Britain would cause the employment of 17 per cent. more workers than those in actual employment in September, 1932. In the woollen industry 13 per cent. more would be employed, in the worsted industry 15 per cent. more, in the boot and shoe industry 11 per cent., and in the pottery industry 10 per cent. These figures assume that overtime and short time would continue to be worked to the same extent as before, but it must be remembered that the calculations are only theoretical, and do not take into

[1] *The Times*, June 12th, 1933.
[2] *Hours of Work and Unemployment*, p. 41.

account the possible effects of the shorter working week on production costs.

A practical approach to the 40-hour week, without reduction of wages, has already been made by a few firms in Great Britain. A firm of paint and varnish manufacturers in 1932 established a five-day week of 40 hours instead of the previous 47 hours, at the same rate of wages.[1] The firm adopted this measure because " it considers it inevitable in all rationalised undertakings." A glass works employing over 4,000 workers in August, 1933, reduced the hours of work of shift workers from 45 or 48 to 42 per week, and of day workers from $46\frac{1}{2}$ to $42\frac{1}{2}$ hours, with practically no change of wages.[2] A firm of engineers, employing 1,100 workers, reduced hours from 47 to $41\frac{1}{4}$, without reduction of wages.[3]

Though the instances quoted are isolated ones, they are sufficient to indicate that the question of reduction is being seriously considered by a number of employers. Still, it must be admitted that the usual attitude is that voiced by Sir Herbert Austin at a debate of works managers, directors and foremen, when he maintained that the introduction of a shorter working week would leave the industry of this country in a decidedly worse state than it is at present.[4] He said further " How could it be supposed that we can retain our vital export markets in view of the rising production costs which must inevitably follow ? How should we retain our own markets without a high tariff wall ? "

The industrial conditions in the United States are very different from those in Great Britain, for there a high tariff wall already exists, and it would probably be raised still farther if it were found that home manufactured goods were being ousted to a substantial extent by imported

[1] *Industrial and Labour Information*, 44, p. 106.
[2] *The Times*, Aug. 24th, 1933.
[3] *Op. cit.*, Aug. 19th, 1933.
[4] *Op. cit.*, Sept. 25th, 1933.

goods. The field is, therefore, more suited for the drastic reductions in hours of work, without reduction of wages, which the President has recently inaugurated under the autocratic powers given him by the Industrial Recovery Act. A code of " fair competition " in the cotton textile industry was signed by the President on July 9th, 1933, which establishes a maximum working week of 40 hours, and prohibits the employment of persons under 16 years of age. The use of productive machinery in any mill is limited to a maximum of two shifts totalling 40 hours each per week, and the scheme has the effect of increasing the average wages in the textile industry by about 30 per cent., and reducing working hours by more than 25 per cent.[1]

On July 27th the President signed a shipbuilding code which was much more drastic than the cotton mills code, as it included the substitution of a 32-hour week on all naval work and an average 36-hour week for other work. The minimum wage rate is to be 35 cents an hour in the south and 45 cents in the north. In consequence of this high wage rate, the lowest bids made for the construction of new warships showed an increase of 10 to 20 per cent. over the official estimates.[2] On September 18th the President signed the coal code, which provides for a 40-hour week in the bituminous coal industry, and fixes basic minimum wages.[3] Codes have recently been signed in other industries ; but a permanent code has not yet been secured in the oil industry, though a 40-hour week, at a minimum wage of 40 to 52 cents, has been arranged for.[4] The codes already signed apply for short periods only, so no sort of finality can yet be assumed for any of them.

The most recent information obtainable states[5] that a

[1] *The Times*, July 11th, 1933.
[2] *Op. cit.*, July 28th, 1933.
[3] *Op. cit.*, Sept. 19th, 1933.
[4] *Op. cit.*, Aug. 11th, 1933.
[5] *Internat. Lab. Rev.*, 29, p. 84, 1934.

40-hour week has now been introduced among employees in the following occupations and industries: clerical work, banking, office work; in shops such as shoe stores and retail dry goods stores; among those engaged in the production of clothing, underwear, textiles (cotton and wool), rayon, hosiery, boots and shoes, furniture, hardware, automobiles, electrical appliances, timber, petroleum, coal, iron and steel; and in over 180 other industries and trades.

A 36-hour week has been introduced in cement and glass manufacture, as well as in the shipbuilding industry previously mentioned.

It is maintained[1] that the National Recovery Administration, under which the alterations of hours and of other conditions have been established, has transformed the industrial structure of American society. Destructive competition and unhealthy trading practices have been eliminated, child labour has been stamped out, and sweated labour has been very largely got rid of. Five-sixths of the 24,000,000 workers engaged in industrial pursuits have already been brought under permanent codes of fair competition, and it is expected that very shortly the whole of American industry will have been brought into the new system. The employers as a class have come to value highly the advantages proceeding from the better organisation, and have found that the greater efficiency engendered has gone far to offset the increase in labour costs caused by the establishment of minimum rates and maximum hours of work. Organised labour, on the other hand, though well aware of the vast improvement in the conditions of employment, does not consider that the N.R.A. has gone far enough.

[1] *The Times*, Jan. 25th, 1934.

OVERHEAD COSTS

The main objection of the employers to the adoption of a 40-hour week depends upon its influence on overhead costs. At the International Labour Conference held at Geneva in 1932 some of the employers stated that the 40-hour week would raise the cost of production 15 or even 20 per cent., and at the Conference held in January, 1933, a French employer stated that it would increase costs by something between 10 and 18 per cent. It is clear that the question of overhead costs is fundamentally important, so it is necessary to enquire into it in some detail.

Overhead costs are generally considered to cover all the costs of production except those of raw materials and direct labour. They include capital charges in the form of interest on loans and rent of land; rates and taxes; insurance and workmen's compensation; depreciation of buildings and depreciation of plant from obsolescence and exposure; storekeeping, and factory office expenses. All of these charges continue in almost undiminished degree whatever the hours of work in force. Other overhead costs such as maintenance of plant and tools, factory supervision, power, light, water and heating, vary to some extent with the hours of work, though not proportionately to them. The exact delimitation and determination of these and other charges is almost impossible, and it is usual to group them together under a single figure which is sometimes called " other expenses."

Information concerning Great Britain was reported to the Committee on Industry and Trade (the " Balfour Committee ") by one or two firms in twenty different industries.[1] It stated that the " other expenses " were greater than, or equal to, wages and salaries in under-

[1] Quoted from *Report on New Aspects of the Problem of Hours of Work*, p. 26.

THE WEEKLY HOURS NOW WORKED

takings manufacturing pig-iron, steel ingots, chemical and coke. They were less than wages and salaries, but not less than one-third of them, in undertakings concerned in general engineering, electrical engineering, cotton spinning and gas manufacture. They were less than one-

PERCENTAGE DISTRIBUTION OF COSTS OF PRODUCTION IN SELECTED INDUSTRIES

Industry.	Materials.	Wages and salaries.	Overhead costs.	Overheads as per cent. on wages, etc.
	Per cent.	Per cent	Per cent.	Per cent.
Fuel production:				
Coal-mining	10·3	74·3	15·4	21
Coke-making	85·2	8·3	6·5	78
Gas	12·9	46·1	41·0	89
Iron and steel:				
Steel ingots	79·3	7·6	13·1	172
Basic pig-iron	80·9	8·7	10·4	120
Hæmatite pig-iron	82·9	10·6	6·5	61
Wire	67·9	21·1	11·0	52
Engineering:				
Pedal bicycles	34·7	37·6	27·7	74
Agricultural machinery	37·0	37·7	25·3	67
Locomotives	46·0	36·0	18·0	50
Electrical engineering	42·5	28·5	29·0	102
Shipbuilding (hulls only)	60·5	33·3	6·2	19
Chemicals (soap)	79·9	10·1	10·0	99
Boots and shoes	57·2	26·6	16·2	61
Cotton-spinning (Egyptian)	74·4	16·2	9·4	58
Cotton-weaving (printers' cloth)	78·5	18·7	2·8	15

third of wages and salaries in undertakings concerned in coal-mining, shipbuilding, cotton-weaving, and the manufacture of boots and shoes, hosiery and clothing. More exact data are supplied by the International Labour Office in their report on " Hours of Work and Unemployment,"[1] and the data relating to the post-war period

[1] P. 197.

(in Great Britain) are reproduced, with slight modification, in the table. It will be seen that they record, as percentages, the distribution of costs of production between materials, wages and salaries, and overhead costs. The overhead costs for the most part bear a similar relationship to wages and salaries to that indicated by the Balfour Committee, the chief exceptions being observed in coke manufacture, which has distinctly lower costs than that indicated by the Committee, and in boot and shoe manufacture, which has double the overhead costs indicated by the Committee.

The overhead costs observed in American industries, so far as comparable data exist,[1] resemble those observed in Great Britain. Thus in coal-mining they were found (in 1918) to be 21 per cent. of the labour costs, and in shoe manufacture, 56 per cent. of them. However, the cost of manufacturing grey sheeting and blue denim cloth was 89 per cent. of the labour costs, a very different figure from that quoted (for a different class of cloth) in the above table.

In some industries, such as building and quarrying, the overhead costs are very much smaller than in the manufacturing industries, but taking industry as a whole it seems probable that the total overhead costs amount to about half the direct labour cost. Florence[2] considers them to be equal to the labour cost, and Lord Leverhulme,[3] in his book on " The Six-Hour Day," states that in most workshops and factories the cost of production in the form of overhead charges is double or more the cost of wages. He says that in the textile industries it is about equal to the wages, but he gives no numerical details. Admittedly our information is not sufficient to enable us to make more than a very rough guess, but the con-

[1] Florence, P. S., *Economics of Fatigue and Unrest*, London, 1924, p. 134.
[2] *L.c.* p. 135.
[3] Leverhulme, *The Six-Hour Day*, London, 1918, p. 19.

clusions of the Balfour Committee, coupled with the contents of the table on page 71, seem to me to support the lower estimate I have suggested.

SHIFT SYSTEMS

As it is evident that the costs of production tend to rise when the hours of work are reduced, owing to the dead weight of the overhead charges, the question naturally arises—Why not run the plant for even longer hours than at present, but reduce the hours of work of the individual workmen, *i.e.*, why not adopt a shift system ? On the absolutely continuous system followed in a few industries (*e.g.*, pig-iron production in blast furnaces) the plant is kept running for 168 hours per week, while in the semi-continuous industries (*e.g.*, steel and tin-plate production), in which work usually ceases on Saturday afternoons and on Sundays, it runs 128 to 136 hours. In 1918 Lord Leverhulme propounded his scheme for a six-hour day at the full weekly wage.[1] A continuous shift system was suggested, according to which the first shift would work from 7 a.m. to 1.15 p.m., with a 15-minute interval for breakfast, *i.e.*, they would work six hours a day for six days, or 36 hours a week. The afternoon shift would work from 1.15 to 9 p.m., with half-an-hour's interval for tea, *i.e.*, they would work $7\frac{1}{4}$ hours a day from Monday to Thursday, but on Friday they would stop at 8.45 p.m., and as Saturday afternoon would be free, they would likewise be working 36 hours a week. The night shift, when one had to be worked, would run from 10 p.m. to 6 a.m., or for 8 hours, as it is inconvenient for a man's household to be disturbed between these hours. The men would be compensated for the relatively long nights

---

[1] Leverhulme, *l.c.*; also *The Organiser*, April and May, 1918; *The Glasgow Herald*, March 29th, 1918.

by being asked to work them only one week in four, and having to put in 5⅓ hours by day in the other three weeks. Thereby the average 36 hours per week would be maintained.

This scheme was found to be impracticable, and as far as I am aware no part of it was ever installed either at the soap works at Port Sunlight or anywhere else. An approach to it has recently been made in a section of the Billingham works of Imperial Chemical Industries.[1] Certain of the shops which hitherto worked the normal 47-hour week of day work were put on to continuous shift work. Four six-hour shifts were arranged, the total hours of work, including Sundays, averaging rather less than 40 per week. As night work is more highly paid than day work, it was possible to pay the men the same wages for the short working week as before. This new arrangement applies to about 15 per cent. of the total number of workpeople employed.

It will be gathered that a shift system can conveniently consist of two shifts following immediately on one another and worked during the day and evening, or it can consist of three or four successive shifts which follow one another throughout the 24 hours, and in some instances continue over the week-end. Women are forbidden by law to work by night, but they are allowed, by special arrangement, to work two shifts between the hours of 6 a.m. and 10 p.m. We shall see that they usually work for 7½ hours in each shift, with half an hour's break in the middle, and as no work is done on Saturday afternoon they keep the plant running for 82½ hours a week. This is a tremendous increase on the usual 48-hour week, and even if the hours were reduced to 6½ per shift, whereby work might be arranged to start at 7 a.m. and cease at 9 p.m., the plant would still be kept running for 71½ hours a week. If, as the result of the increasing productivity of labour, 5 hours'

[1] *The Times*, Oct. 12th, 1933.

work per day were found to be sufficient to provide all our needs, it would be most economical to run three successive shifts each day (*e.g.*, from 6.30 a.m. to 9.30 p.m.), and with one shift on Saturday the plant would be kept running for 80 hours a week. If eventually four-hour shifts were found to be an economic possibility, four of them could be arranged to run consecutively from 6 a.m. to 10 p.m. on Monday to Friday, and two (from 6 a.m. to 2 p.m.) on Saturday. Thereby the plant would be kept running for 88 hours per week. Alternatively, if there were three of these 4-hour shifts per day and two on Saturday, the plant would be kept running for 68 hours per week.

The adoption of a shift system is of greater and greater economic importance the higher the ratio of overhead costs to labour costs. Let us take as a contrast the electrical engineering and the cotton weaving industries mentioned in the last table. In the former industry the overhead costs were 102 per cent. on the labour costs, and in the latter, 15 per cent. Supposing that the workmen in each industry were paid 100 shillings for a 48-hour week, it would follow that the overhead costs for each hour of work would be 2·1 shillings and 0·3 shilling respectively. If, however, a two-shift system were adopted, with $82\frac{1}{2}$ hours of work per week, the overhead costs would drop to 1·2 and 0·2 shillings per hour respectively, *i.e.*, the saving would be 0·9 shilling in one case, and only 0·1 shilling in the other. Conversely, if a 40-hour week were adopted instead of the usual 48-hour week, the overhead costs per hour would rise to 2·55 shillings in the electrical engineering industry and to 0·4 shilling in the weaving industry ; *i.e.*, by 0·45 and 0·1 shilling respectively. Employers in the former industry would therefore be specially disinclined to adopt the 40-hour week, and specially inclined to adopt the two-shift system. Industry as a whole tends to become more and more mechanised, and to show a steady increase of overhead costs in relation to direct labour costs, so an increasingly powerful argument is afforded against the adoption of a shorter working week unless it is based on a shift system.

It will be realised that a shift system, once it is substituted for the ordinary day work, is so elastic and adaptable that the total hours for which the plant is run per week can easily be maintained at a very much higher figure than under the present system. Thereby the dead weight of overhead costs may be so substantially reduced that the employers can afford to pay the same wages for the shorter working week as for the 48-hour week. Especially does this argument hold for the more mechanised industries with their high overhead costs. A regulated two-shift system with shifts of 7 or $7\frac{1}{2}$ hours' duration has been developing gradually in Great Britain since the war, and is described fully in the next four chapters.[1] This system applies only to women and young persons, for men, when working on shifts, are not bound by special regulations. Nevertheless, men work in conjunction with women in a very large number of industries, so it follows that many of them will be affected by the regulated system. Ultimately most of them may conform to it.

[1] *Cf.*, Vernon, H. M., *Internat. Lab. Rev.*, 29, p. 165, 1934.

CHAPTER IV

THE TWO-SHIFT SYSTEM

CONTENTS

Introduction—The Procedure Adopted in Granting Two-Shift Orders—The Numbers of Orders Granted and Workers Involved—The Reasons for Obtaining Orders—The Hours of Work

INTRODUCTION

DURING the Great War very large numbers of women were working in munition factories by night as well as by day, either on two-shift or three-shift systems, and sometimes, when night work was not necessary, they worked on two 8-hour day shifts. After the war, when most of these munition women had been discharged and there was a period of booming trade and high pressure in manufacture, it was considered that, though the night shift should undoubtedly be abolished, it was worth while to continue two day shifts so long as they did not extend beyond the hours of 6 a.m. and 10 p.m. A Departmental Committee of the Home Office held an extended enquiry on the subject, during the 14 sittings of which no less than 129 witnesses were examined.[1] They included representatives selected by women who were actually employed on the two-shift system in various works, representatives of organised labour, employers' organisations, Joint Industrial Councils, the Factory Department of the Home Office, the Board of Education, the Ministry of Labour, and in addition medical witnesses and social workers.

[1] Report by Departmental Committee on Employment of Women and Young Persons on the Two-Shift System, *Cmd.* 1037, 1920.

Some of the witnesses said that the alternation of shifts, with consequent disturbance of the hours for food and rest, led to sleeplessness, digestive disorders and general deterioration. The early and late hours, often resulting in scamped meals, were said to cause undue strain. The women on morning shift sometimes spent most of the afternoon in doing housework, and similarly the women on afternoon shift worked during the morning. The result was that they were robbed of their proper recreation and came tired to their work. However, the medical evidence, and that of the welfare workers and the majority of the factory inspectors interrogated, did not indicate any adverse influence on health.

It was stated that the women and young persons on two shifts were deprived of the advantages of club life and evening classes, but it was pointed out by the Committee that the attendance at such classes, even under the most favourable conditions, is very small in proportion to the number of women employed in industry. Another objection pressed upon the Committee was the disturbance which the two-shift system caused to family life. It was said that the mother of the family, or housewife, was kept incessantly at work preparing meals at all hours of the day and night, and that the family was robbed of the comfort and happiness of a common table. However, competent witnesses informed the Committee that actual experience showed that the objections to the provision of meals were not so great nor so widespread as was suggested. They said that the housewife did not usually get up to provide breakfast before the 6 o'clock start, or remain up to provide supper at night, and the Committee concluded that little if any difficulty is experienced in making arrangements for meals.

The Committee unanimously concluded that though the experience of the two-shift system was limited, and the whole question had not yet passed out of the experimental stage, a case was made out for allowing the adoption of the system under certain conditions. They accordingly suggested that the system might be adopted for a limited period of five years, at the end of which Parliament would be free to review the whole question and decide whether the system should be continued for a further period, or abandoned.

In 1920 an Act termed " The Employment of Women, Young Persons and Children Act " was passed through Parliament after some opposition by members of the Labour Party. Under Section 2 of this Act the Secretary of State for the Home Department was given power to grant Orders authorising the employment of women and young persons over 16 between the hours of 6 a.m. and 10 p.m. on any week-day except Saturday, and between 6 a.m. and 2 p.m. on Saturday, on two shifts averaging not more than eight hours each.

In a debate on the two-shift system held in 1926 [1] Mr. Rhys Davies asked if the Home Secretary (Sir W. Joynson Hicks) would cause an enquiry to be held into the operation of the two-shift system in order to determine whether it might be necessary to continue the Act in the Schedule of the next Expiring Laws Continuance Bill. The Home Secretary said in reply that the operation of the system had been carefully watched by the Factory Department ever since its inception, and that it was one of the duties of the Women Deputy Superintending Inspectors in particular to make a special study of the question. The results of the investigations were on the whole favourable to the system, and provision had been made for its continuance in Clause 74 of the Factories Bill.

As the Factories Bill has never been passed, the Act authorising the two-shift system has to be renewed every year under the Expiring Laws Continuance Bill. This renewal affords an occasion for debate, and on several

[1] *Hansard*, Vol. 199, H.C., p. 157.

occasions some of the Labour members have taken full advantage of their opportunity. Reference to these debates is made in a subsequent chapter.

THE PROCEDURE ADOPTED IN GRANTING TWO-SHIFT ORDERS

The Workers' Consent.—When a firm wishes to place some of its employees under the two-shift system, it has to make a joint application to the Home Office in which a majority of the workpeople affected by the Order have signified their consent. The subsequent proceedings are best indicated by quoting from a speech made in Parliament by the Home Secretary (Sir W. Joynson Hicks).[1] He said: "An inspector goes down to the factory. In many cases a meeting of the workers is held and a full discussion takes place with them. The inspector explains to them what the two-shift system involves, and discusses with them what extra welfare arrangements will be needed, and enquires what are the arrangements for the transport of the workers in the case of girls who have to start work early or go home late. He enquires whether there are buses or trams available, or whether it is necessary to insist on a particular form of transport being provided by the firm. He has to be satisfied and has to report to me that a majority of the workers are definitely in favour of the scheme before I can even entertain the idea of granting an Order. He has to be satisfied that the workers have given their opinion voluntarily without any pressure from the employers."

It must be admitted that in some instances indirect pressure is brought to bear on the workers. Some firms, when engaging fresh employees, ask them if they are prepared to work on shifts if required to do so. As there

[1] *Hansard*, Vol. 222, H.C., Nov. 16th, 1928.

may be no immediate prospect of the shift system being adopted the employees usually do not trouble to weigh the future possibilities to which they are committing themselves. At one works a definite clause relating to shift work was incorporated in the form of application for employment. In a few instances the women have been led to understand that failure to acquiesce will sooner or later result in discharge from the factory, and replacement by other and more amenable workers.

Mr. Rhys Davies, during the course of a parliamentary debate on the two-shift system, even went so far as to state that " It has been proved beyond doubt that the ballot in some cases is nothing but a farce. If any workpeople give an indication of opposition the employer can at once find some excuse for dispensing with their services, thereby facilitating his obtaining the Order. The will of the employer therefore in practically every case is dominant." Nevertheless, the obligation of the employer to consult his workers before introducing the system is a useful check, which in some instances has definitely prevented the adoption of the system. For instance, in one factory, where an Order applying to 1,800 workers was sought, it had to be given up as only 400 signatures out of the necessary 901 could be obtained.

The Order, once obtained, appears to remain in force permanently, provided that the above-mentioned annual renewal of the Act under the Expiring Laws Continuance Bill is passed. As many of the workers who signed the original application inevitably drop out from time to time, they are replaced by others who took no part in it, and who have no real choice in the matter. They may be new workers who were not even told that they were to work on a shift system when they were engaged. Also it is permissible to increase the numbers of workers above that specified in the application, and in many instances this increase has been so considerable that factory inspectors have had to point out that, even if the letter of the regulation is complied with, an offence is being committed against its spirit. As is mentioned in a subsequent chapter, many Orders are used intermittently, and of the workers put on to shift work when the Order is revived few if any may have taken part in the original application. The Orders now issued by the Home Office contain a proviso that the inspectorate should be notified when the use of an Order is revived after its temporary suspension, but this condition is not always complied with.

The Orders granted apply only to the particular industrial processes stipulated, and if an employer desires to apply the system to other processes it is necessary for him to obtain a fresh Order. Also it applies only to the particular factory mentioned, and cannot be used if the workers concerned are transferred elsewhere, *e.g.*, to a branch factory of the same firm.

The Provisions of the Order.—The Order granted contains a number of provisions and stipulations, which vary a good deal according to the circumstances under which it was made. For instance, if an Order is granted in an emergency caused by a factory being partly destroyed by fire, it would obviously defeat one of the most valuable applications of the two-shift system if such a proviso as full messroom and cloakroom accommodation were insisted upon. If such accommodation were lacking it might take weeks or months to install. Under ordinary circumstances, however, the factory inspectorate make a careful investigation of the available accommodation, and if they consider it to be inadequate it has to be raised to the requisite standard before the Order is granted. The cloakroom accommodation should provide facilities for drying damp clothing, and the washing arrangements should be adequate. As the shift workers have almost invariably to eat their meals on the premises, it is important that they should be provided with a suitable messroom, supplied with facilities for warming food, or still better, with proper canteens. At quite a number of factories the messroom and cloakroom accommodation for the ordinary day-shift workers has been improved considerably owing to the requirements demanded for the shift workers, and the welfare supervision has likewise been improved.

The Orders are made subject to any conditions which the Secretary of State may see fit to impose " for the purpose of safeguarding the welfare of the persons employed," and reference is frequently made in subsequent pages to various welfare provisions. They were summarised[1] by the Home Secretary (Sir W. Joynson Hicks) in 1928 in the following terms: " In nearly every case I make Orders of a special character in regard to welfare, the provision of cloakrooms, messroom accommodation, washing facilities, protective clothing, seats for workers and transport facilities."

The Orders apply to girls and boys aged 16 to 18, as well as to women of 18 and upwards, but where girls are concerned an additional stipulation is made that a welfare supervisor or forewoman should be available who will see that the welfare conditions are properly carried out.

Transport.—Special attention is paid to the question of transport, for this is often a very important consideration to workers living at a distance from the factory. The early shift generally start work at 6 a.m., and at this hour the usual bus and tram services may not be running, or may be inadequate. Almost all the employers appear to be fully alive to the transport difficulty, and they endeavour to overcome it by arranging to put on to shifts only the workers who live in the neighbourhood, or those who can come fairly easily by cycle or by public conveyance. If such conveyances are lacking they may approach the railway and bus companies and get them to provide greater facilities, or they may install a private bus service of their

[1] *Hansard*, Vol. 222, Nov. 16th, 1928.

own. Sometimes, when the train or bus service is inadequate and the companies concerned are unable to improve it, the employers allow the shift workers to arrive late for their work, or to leave early. Cases have been noted where they came from 15 to 40 minutes late in the morning; in others, they left 10 minutes before the shift ended.

Sometimes a condition is inserted in the Order requiring the employer to make special arrangements for the conveyance of workers living at a distance. Again, the workers have in some cases made their consent conditional on a clause being inserted requiring adequate arrangements to be made.[1]

Very elaborate arrangements for transport have been made at a large artificial silk factory situated about three miles outside a big town in the Midlands. The welfare supervisor, when engaging an employee, notes her address on a card index, and fills in details of the transport arrangements for the district involved. Fleets of buses feed all suitable areas, and take the workers backwards and forwards. In all 50 or 60 buses were running (in 1928), each containing about 30 workers. They were used by the men on the three-shift system as well as by the two-shift women. So far as possible, no worker was taken on to shift work if she had to leave home before 5 a.m., or return after 11 p.m. Failing these conditions she was transferred to day work. If the shift workers did not come by bus details were entered on the index cards as to times of starting from home and of returning, and the length of journey on foot, cycle or train.

An investigation on the two-shift system was made in 1925 by two investigators[2] attached to the Industrial Fatigue Research Board, and a report on their work is

---

[1] Report of Chief Inspector of Factories for 1929, p. 54.
[2] Smith, May and Vernon, M. D., Report No. 47 of Indust. Fatigue Research Board, pp. 17-30, 1928.

frequently referred to in subsequent pages. They collected information about the times of transport at the artificial silk factory in question, and at three other factories, devoted to electrical engineering, paper bag manufacture and wire manufacture respectively. This information is recorded statistically in the table, and it

TIMES TAKEN IN TRANSIT FROM HOME TO FACTORY (TWO-SHIFT WORKERS)

Minutes.	Artificial silk factory.	Electrical engineering factory.	Paper-bag factory.	Wire-drawing factory.	Average.
	%	%	%	%	%
0–10	3	12	65	13	23
10–20	9	36	25	39	27
20–30	18	36	10	44	27
30–40	26	16	0	4	12
40–50	31	0	0	0	8
50–60	9	0	0	0	2
Over 60	5	0	0	0	1
Median time in minutes	38	21	9	19	
Number of workers involved	1821	50	40	23	

will be seen that of the 1,821 shift workers questioned at the silk factory the majority took 30 to 50 minutes to get from their homes to the factory. A small number, 5 per cent., took over 60 minutes at the time the enquiry was made, but this was only for a temporary period. At the other three factories the great majority of the workers took less than 30 minutes to get to their work. These times compare favourably with the times observed in the course of another investigation made upon ordinary day workers,[1] for it will be seen from the data in the table that at one factory 31 per cent. of them took 60 to 74 minutes. The " median " times recorded are the " middlemost "

TIMES TAKEN IN TRANSIT FROM HOME TO FACTORY (DAY-WORKERS)

Minutes taken.	Percentage of workers taking various times at	
	Factory A.	Factory B.
Less than 15 minutes	7	15
15–29 minutes	4	29
30–44 ,,	24	40
45–59 ,,	34	11
60–74 ,,	31	4
75–115 ,,	0	1
Median time in minutes	52	32
Numbers of workers investigated	235	586

times, or such times that half of all the observations made fall below them in magnitude, and half above them.

The provision of special transport for two-shift workers has occasionally resulted in ill-feeling on the part of the ordinary day-shift workers who were not provided with such facilities. At one factory they were apt to hurl abuse at the shift workers as they drove past.

THE NUMBERS OF ORDERS GRANTED AND WORKERS INVOLVED

The Number of Orders Granted.—The number of Orders granted each year is usually mentioned in the annual

[1] Vernon, H. M., Vernon, M. D., and Lorrain-Smith, I., Report No. 47 of Indust. Fatigue Research Board, pp. 1–16, 1928.

THE TWO-SHIFT SYSTEM

reports of the Chief Inspector of Factories. It is stated[1] that at the end of 1922, or two years after the Act had been in force, 235 Orders had been granted, of which about half were in use. At the end of 1924, 425 Orders had been granted, of which about a third were in use.[2] During the next five years fresh Orders were granted at the rate of about 100 a year, and in the 1929 Report a detailed analysis is given of the Orders in existence.[3] Up to the end of June, 1929, they were 852 in number, and had been granted to 653 firms in respect of 750 works; but 168 of them had become permanently inoperative, either through the works having been closed down or the Orders having been superseded by later ones, and 351, though still in operation, were not thought likely to be used again. Of the remaining 333 Orders, representing 39 per cent. on the total granted, 191 were used intermittently but were considered likely to be helpful in the future, while 142 were used more or less continuously.

In 1930, and in the first eight months of 1931, the number of Orders showed a slight rise, but in the last four months of 1931 they shot up to about three times those previously granted, owing to the abandonment of the gold standard in September, 1931. The consequent depreciation of sterling resulted in a decrease of imports and a rush of orders in certain home industries, especially in worsted spinning and hosiery. Manufacturers found it necessary to increase production rapidly in order to fulfil orders already in hand and to secure new contracts for goods previously imported, for which early delivery was essential. Out of the 120 Orders granted after the abandonment of the gold standard, 99 were required for one or other of these reasons.[4]

---

[1] Annual Report of Chief Inspector of Factories for 1922, p. 52.
[2] Annual Report for 1924, p. 50.
[3] Annual Report for 1929, p. 54.
[4] Annual Report for 1931, p. 53.

The number of Orders granted during each three-month period in 1929–31 is shown in the table.

The numbers of Orders granted in the eight months

Year.	Jan. 1st to Mar. 31st.	Apr. 1st to June 30th.	July 1st to Sept. 30th.	Oct. 1st to Dec. 31st.	Total.
1929 ...	24	26	32	31	113
1930 ...	26	29	43	31	129
1931 ...	29	43	48	107	227

before the abandonment of the gold standard and in the subsequent ten months are plotted out in Fig. 6.[1] It will

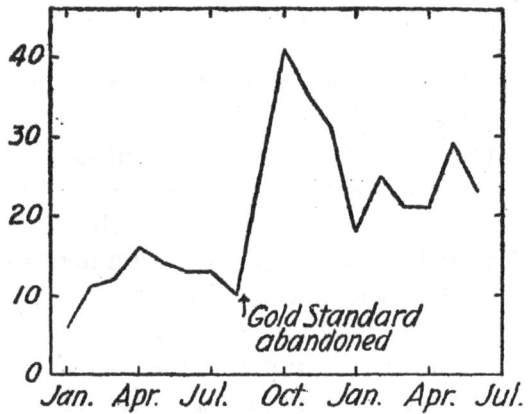

FIG. 6.—Orders granted per month before and after the abandonment of the gold standard.

be seen that they rose to a maximum in October, 1931, and then fell gradually, but throughout 1932 they remained considerably higher than they had been before October, 1931. Judging from the various figures quoted in reports, the total number of Orders in force at the end of 1932 must have amounted to about 1,560.

[1] Cf., *The London Gazette* for 1931 and 1932.

The Number of Workers Involved.—It is impossible to ascertain at all accurately the number of women, girls and boys working under two-shift Orders, because the factories are not asked to make returns of these numbers. Even if they did so they would not be reliable, as the numbers are liable to change rapidly from week to week and from season to season, owing to the large number of Orders which are used intermittently. The Annual Report of the Chief Inspector for 1924 states[1] that the total number of persons employed at any time from January, 1921, to December, 1924, is 22,915, of whom 15,609 were women, 4,297 were girls of 16 to 18, and 3,009 were boys of 16 to 18; but it must not be thought that the numbers in employment at one and the same time approached anywhere near to these figures.

From time to time the factory inspectors make rough estimates of the numbers of shift-workers in their divisions, and these estimates show very great differences in the extent to which the system has been adopted in various parts of the country. It is most popular in the Midland, Eastern and North-Eastern Divisions,[2] and considerably less so in outlying areas. In London itself it is not popular as the workers usually live too far from the factory, but no information is available to show what proportion of the industrial population in various areas has been put on to shift work. In a Parliamentary debate on the two-shift system, held in 1929, Mr. Clynes, the Home Secretary, stated[3] that "forty thousand workers are directly and indirectly affected by it," but this estimate is necessarily a very vague one, as it is impossible to determine the number of workers indirectly affected with any approach to accuracy. A rough estimate obtained from another source indicated that in 1931 there were probably

---
[1] Annual Report for 1924, p. 52.
[2] Report of Chief Inspector of Factories for 1931, p. 55.
[3] *Hansard*, Vol. 232, H.C., Nov. 26th, 1929.

something like 17,000 persons in all working under two-shift Orders, and it therefore seems likely that in 1933 there were over 20,000 workers under the system. This number is, of course, exclusive of the hundreds of thousands of men who work regularly on two-shift and three-shift systems in continuous processes such as are met with in iron, steel and tinplate production, coal-mining, glass-bottle-making, and other industries.

The Extra Employment Caused by the Two-Shift System.—It would be of great interest to ascertain to what extent the use of the two-shift system has increased employment, but the problem is so complex that even the roughest estimate can be only provisional. Supposing that 20,000 workers are now on the system, it might be maintained that half of them, or 10,000, have obtained employment which they would otherwise have missed; but this conclusion by no means follows. If two-shift Orders had not been available the employers would probably have managed to give work to a portion of the extra women by putting in more machinery. On the other hand, the extra production of the women on the two-shift system may mean additional employment for other women and for men who are engaged on processes linked up with those of the two-shift women, whereby the total number of persons employed is considerably augmented. For instance, the Annual Report of the Chief Inspector for 1931[1] describes an occupier who told an Inspector that "the adoption of the system made the difference between success and failure." He said that the number of his employees had increased from 300 to about 580, and that they were able to manufacture more material than their weaving department could deal with. In consequence they were compelled to employ outside weavers, menders and finishers.

At a large artificial silk factory near Derby where, in 1922, over 1,000 women and girls were employed con-

[1] Annual Report of Chief Inspector of Factories for 1931, p. 57.

THE TWO-SHIFT SYSTEM

tinuously on the two-shift system in the textile processes, the management said[1] that "it would be impossible to carry on without it." At an artificial silk factory situated in another district, 430 extra workers were employed on shift work, and the increased production in the departments served by them allowed for full employment in the spinning section, where men alone were employed. At a third artificial silk factory, 450 extra workers were taken on under the two-shift system, and it was calculated that altogether about 1,400 extra women were employed on two-shift work in the district. Another 700 workers were engaged indirectly. Again, it has been found that in hosiery manufacture the employment of two-shift women on winding and knitting may increase the number of persons—both male and female—employed in all the subsequent making up and finishing processes. It might be thought that some of the shift women displaced men from their jobs, but there is no evidence that this has happened, and the inspectors are alive to such a possibility when the granting of an Order is under consideration.

At a paper mill the firm considered the two-shift system to be absolutely essential, and the employment of 60 men depended entirely on the existence of two shifts of women.

In some instances it was thought that the number of other workers indirectly employed as the result of the two-shift system was greater than that of the shift workers, and the previously-mentioned estimate of Mr. Clynes, who said that forty thousand workers were directly or indirectly affected, supports this view. There can, therefore, be no doubt that the adoption of the shift system does create a great deal of extra employment, both directly and indirectly.

[1] Annual Report for 1922, p. 52.

THE REASONS FOR OBTAINING ORDERS

The reasons given by employers for obtaining Orders are summarised in an Annual Report[1] under the following headings:

(1) It effects a reduction of overhead charges, because buildings and machinery are used for longer periods daily.
(2) Orders can be more readily completed, a very important point especially in connection with shipping orders.
(3) Stocks can be readily maintained, but such heavy stocks need not be carried in view of increased rate of production.
(4) Whereas ordinary overtime working is expensive, both on account of the higher rates of wages and the decreased rate of production due to fatigue of the workers, urgent orders can be dealt with by the two-shift system without these extra charges.
(5) When undertaking the manufacture of new classes of goods a smaller capital outlay on machinery and plant is required before production is started, and also before the demand for the particular goods can be known or estimated.
(6) The system is employed in other countries and is necessary in this country in order to be able to make goods at competitive prices.

Other reasons given in the Report[2] are that Orders are wanted to meet sudden rushes of work and to enable manufacturers to obtain contracts which might otherwise have gone abroad. It is a common experience to meet

---

[1] Annual Report of Chief Inspector of Factories for 1931, p. 57.
[2] *L.c.* pp. 53, 54.

with alternations of depression and sudden demand, and the two-shift system is of great assistance in coping with such irregularities. It may be equally so to old-established firms—suffering from shortage of room and plant—who cannot expand because of the situation of their works. Again, it is pointed out that Orders are very useful to tide over the time necessary for the installation of new plant and to meet cases of temporary dislocation through breakdown of machinery or destruction of premises by fire. It may be necessary to adapt existing machinery to new processes, or to reorganise and expand. Some firms have bottle-neck departments which fail to keep pace with other sections when they have a busy season, unless they temporarily adopt the two-shift system. In one instance it was necessary to make up for time lost in a trade dispute, and in another, when a firm of hosiery manufacturers had got behind with their orders owing to deliveries of faulty yarn.

Orders are very useful in seasonal trade such as vegetable and fruit-canning, and the manufacture of ice-cream wafers, whilst tin-box factories allied to the canning industry may also need the shift system.

Some other reasons have been adduced in earlier Reports. For instance, it was pointed out[1] that seasonal pressure in trades such as soap and glue manufacture, in which high temperature affects the product, has been successfully met by taking advantage of the cooler hours in the morning and evening by means of a two-shift Order. Still again, the system is of value in industries with continuous processes, such as are met with in the manufacture of sugar, glass and paper. Here women and young persons may work on two shifts in conjunction with men working on three shifts.

An instance of reduction of overhead charges effected by the adoption of the system is given in the Report of the

[1] Annual Report for 1924, p. 50.

Departmental Committee.[1] It was stated by a witness that in the rubber trade the plant is expensive, and the stocks which have to be carried are very large. The result is that " the turnover in our rubber factory is very little more than equal to the capital engaged. We do not turn over our capital much more than once a year. That is a very low percentage of performance, and in order to turn it over more than that we must increase the output per machine. . . . The only way I can see of meeting that condition is that we should work longer hours . . . by working shifts."

Some employers state that in such industries as artificial silk and hosiery manufacture fashions are apt to change very quickly, and unless the delivery of orders is made in the stipulated time they are cancelled without hesitation. The time limit given allows no margin, so the full utilisation of the plant, by the adoption of the two-shift system, is a necessity.

There can be no doubt that the two-shift system frequently fulfils a very real need, and that its prohibition would entail considerable hardship both on employers and employed. Many of the employers who use their Orders at infrequent intervals would be very loath to give up the privilege, as they realise that they have the system to fall back upon in times of unexpected emergency. It generally takes a week or more to obtain a fresh Order, and such an interval of delay may cause a serious disarrangement of production, and entail a loss of work.

THE HOURS OF WORK

The Usual Hours of Work.—The usual hours of work adopted on the two-shift system are, for the morning shift,

[1] Report of Departmental Co. on Employment of Women and Young Persons on Two-Shift System, *Cmd.* 1037, 1920, p. 6.

THE TWO-SHIFT SYSTEM

6 a.m. to 2 p.m. on every morning from Monday to Saturday, and for the afternoon shift, 2 p.m. to 10 p.m. on Monday to Friday. No work is permitted by law after 2 p.m. on Saturday, and the afternoon shift, after completing their shift on the Friday evening, are not allowed to do any more work on the Saturday morning. They are, therefore, strictly limited to five shifts a week, but as the shifts have to change over every week it is more accurate to say that all shift-workers work eleven shifts per fortnight. A meal break of at least half an hour's duration must be taken, and as no work spell of more than 5 hours (or $4\frac{1}{2}$ hours in textile industries) is permitted, it means that the breakfast interval must be taken some time between 8.30 a.m. and 11 a.m. Usually it is taken at 9.0 to 9.30 a.m., while the tea interval is taken at 5.30 to 6.0 p.m. Hence the work spells are usually:

Morning shift: 6 to 9 and 9.30 to 2, or for 3 and $4\frac{1}{2}$ hours respectively.
Afternoon shift: 2 to 5.30 and 6 to 10, or for $3\frac{1}{2}$ and 4 hours respectively.

These hours add up to 45 and $37\frac{1}{2}$ per week for the two shifts, or to $41\frac{1}{4}$ hours on an average, and are, therefore, considerably less than the 47 or 48 hours worked per week by most of those employed on the ordinary day-shift.

In textile factories in textile districts it is the usual practice to cease work at noon on Saturdays, and in that case the morning shift would work 43 hours a week instead of 45 hours, while the average hours would fall to $40\frac{1}{4}$ per week.

Abbreviated Hours of Work.—In a few factories the duration of each shift is reduced from 8 hours (including the meal-time) to $7\frac{1}{2}$ or 7 hours by starting later than 6 a.m., or by finishing earlier than 10 p.m. For instance, at a margarine factory the shifts ran from 7 a.m. to 2.30

p.m., and 2.30 to 10 p.m., the meal break being at 10 to 10.30 a.m. and 6 to 6.30 p.m. At a canister works the hours ran from 6 a.m. to 1.30 p.m. and 1.30 to 9 p.m.; at another factory, from 6.30 a.m. to 2 p.m. and 2 p.m. to 9.30 p.m. At these factories the working week of the two shifts was, therefore, 42 and 35 hours respectively, or $38\frac{1}{2}$ hours on an average.

Though it is the usual custom for the meal break to last for the minimum statutory period of half an hour, at one factory it was extended to an hour, and the shift-workers accordingly put in only 7 hours of actual work per shift instead of $7\frac{1}{2}$ hours. At another factory the morning shift were given a $\frac{1}{4}$-hour break at 8 a.m. and a $\frac{1}{2}$-hour break at 10 a.m. As the afternoon shift had only the usual $\frac{1}{2}$-hour break, it follows that while they worked the usual $7\frac{1}{2}$ hours per shift and $37\frac{1}{2}$ hours per week, the morning shift worked only $7\frac{1}{4}$ hours per shift or $43\frac{1}{2}$ hours per week.

There is no legal compulsion to make the duration of the shifts of equal length, and one of them may even exceed 8 hours in duration if desired, for the Act merely states that the two shifts may not *average* more than eight hours each. No instance has come to my notice of a shift working for more than eight hours, but there are several instances of unequal hours. At one factory the morning shift worked from 7 a.m. to 2 p.m., or for 39 hours per week instead of the usual 45 hours, while the afternoon shift worked from 2 to 10 p.m., or for the usual $37\frac{1}{2}$ hours per week. At another factory the hours ran from 6 a.m. to 1 p.m., and from 1 to 9 p.m. These schemes had the advantage of nearly equalising the hours of work and the earnings of the women in the alternate weeks, but it reduced the average working week from $41\frac{1}{4}$ hours to $38\frac{1}{4}$ hours. It is not likely that employers would, at the present time, willingly consent to such a reduction of hours, so a more feasible plan of equalisation would be for the afternoon shift to work distinctly longer hours than the morning shift. If the morning shift lasted from 6 a.m. to 1.20 p.m., the hours worked per week would come to 41, and if the afternoon shift lasted from 1.20 to 10 p.m. the hours would come to 40 hours 50 minutes, or would be of practically the same duration.

Exceptional Hours of Work.—Under exceptional circumstances the Home Office has permitted entirely different arrangements of working hours. For instance, at a paper-bag factory the two shifts worked for the following hours on Mondays to Fridays :[1]

First shift : 6.30 to 11.30 and 1.30 to 3.15, or for 5 and $1\frac{3}{4}$ hours respectively.
Second shift : 11.30 to 1.30 and 3.15 to 8, or for 2 and $4\frac{3}{4}$ hours respectively.

On Saturdays the first shift worked from 6.30 to 10.30 a.m., and the second shift from 10.15 a.m. to 2 p.m., so the total hours worked by the two shifts came to $37\frac{3}{4}$ hours and $37\frac{1}{2}$ hours per week respectively. In addition, the first shift sometimes came back to work at 12.45 instead of 1.30 p.m., and the second shift sometimes started at 11.20 a.m. The hours then worked approached in duration the longer ones worked by most shift-workers. It will be noted that under this arrangement the workers got a dinner break lasting $1\frac{3}{4}$ or 2 hours, and the arrangement appeared to find general favour.

At two canning factories each shift of women was allowed to work two spells of 4 hours each, separated by 4-hour intervals, in accordance with the following time schedule :

First shift : 6 to 10 and 2 to 6 on M. to S., or for 48 hours per week.
Second shift : 10 to 2 and 6 to 10 on M. to F., or for 40 hours per week.

[1] Smith, M., and Vernon, M. D., *l.c.*, p. 23.

By this means all loss of time for a dinner interval was avoided, and the women were able to work for 8 hours a day, or for 48 and 40 hours a week respectively on the two shifts. This arrangement of hours was permitted because all the women concerned lived close to the factories.

A more complicated system of shifts is described in the Annual Report for 1928.[1]

> Shift 1: M., W. and F., 7 to 11 and 6 to 10 ; T. and Th., 11 to 6.
> Shift 2: M., W. and F., 11 to 6 ; T. and Th., 7 to 11 and 6 to 10 ; S., 7. to 12.

This system avoids the early 6 a.m. start, and the workers have to finish at 10 p.m. only on two or three evenings a week, but the total hours worked by the two shifts amount only to 37 and $40\frac{1}{2}$ respectively, or $38\frac{3}{4}$ on an average. The workers involved lived close to the factory.

---

[1] Annual Report of Chief Inspector of Factories for 1928, p. 52.

CHAPTER V

THE TWO-SHIFT SYSTEM IN CONTINUOUS OPERATION

CONTENTS

Introduction—Factories Employing the Two-Shift System on a Substantial Scale—Output and Loss of Working Time—The Dependence of Rate of Production on Hours of Work—The Wages Paid—The Influence of the Two-Shift System on Health—The Influence of the Three-Shift System on Health

INTRODUCTION

THE degree of success attainable by the two-shift system can be estimated properly only after it has been in continuous operation for a year or more on a fairly considerable scale. We shall see, in a subsequent chapter, that the adoption of the system inevitably involves such a change of habits that the worker is almost always antagonised at first, and it is only after she has been employed sufficiently long to get accustomed to the system that her opinion of its merits is likely to be at all impartial. Similarly the managers, foremen, and mechanics in charge at a factory have to adapt themselves to the changed conditions, and at first, until the system is properly installed on a substantial scale, they may in many cases have to work overtime. Their numbers cannot be easily and quickly duplicated like those of the shift-workers, and either they have to suffer or the supervision has to be reduced.

It will be best to describe first some of the larger factories where a fairly considerable proportion of the women have been working continuously on the system for a year or more, and subsequently to refer more briefly to a number of industries and occupations where it is running continuously on a small scale. Finally, we shall see that in many factories, both large and small, it is run intermittently owing to seasonal requirements, or temporarily owing to some of the causes referred to in the last chapter.

FACTORIES EMPLOYING THE TWO-SHIFT SYSTEM ON A SUBSTANTIAL SCALE

Textile Factories.—The number of factories where the two-shift system is in continuous operation on a substantial scale is very limited, and the table on page 101 probably records about half of the factories where 50 or more women were working on the system in 1928. I have been unable to obtain adequate statistics for more recent years.

The industry in which the two-shift system has been most fully developed is that relating to the manufacture of artificial silk and its products. This is a comparatively new and rapidly-expanding industry, so its promoters were less likely to be tied by long-established custom and tradition when selecting the conditions of employment of their workers. Again, the expansion of the industry was at one time so rapid that it was difficult—without the adoption of the system—to install and work sufficient machinery to produce the desired output. The system was adopted on the largest and most complete scale at a factory situated about three miles from a big town in the Midlands. For some years about 2,000 women, or the greater number of those employed, were on shift work, but this number has been reduced in recent years owing to smaller demand. The women are employed on a number of different types of work, including (*a*) winding silk from bobbins on to small cardboard spools called pirns ; (*b*) winding silk on to large wooden spools, for hosiery and underwear ; (c) winding silk from bobbins into skeins, for dyeing, and winding the dyed silk on to bobbins for

WOMEN IN CONTINUOUS OCCUPATION UNDER THE TWO-SHIFT SYSTEM

Trade or Occupation.	Number of women on two-shift system.	Percentage on total number of women employed.
Textile and clothing industries :		
Artificial silk, hosiery, underwear	2,000	70
Artificial silk	100	20
Artificial silk	75	25
Hosiery, underwear	250	25
Metal and engineering industries :		
Rolling aluminium plates	100	30
Drawing and galvanising wire	50	40
Electrical engineering	100	20
General engineering	60	30
Miscellaneous industries :		
Sugar-packing	250	20
Margarine-packing	60	5
Yeast-packing (3 factories)	80	93
Rubber tyres	270	18
Rubber tyres	80	7
Cardboard boxes	200	50
Paper bags	60	100
Rope-spinning	120	25
Parqueting	60	15
Candle wicks	70	10

twisting, etc. ; (d) twisting silk from bobbins into thicker strands (chiefly for knitting yarn, to be sold retail) ; (e) sizing the silk and winding it on to the weaver's beam ready for the warp ; (f) weaving the silk ; (g) seaming and welting silk stockings ; (*h*) making up material into underwear, skirts, etc.

Another firm of artificial silk manufacturers had 100 women on shift-work, and a third firm owned several factories, one of which employed 75 shift-workers, and the others about 20 each. A firm manufacturing hosiery and underwear, but not the artificial silk itself, had 250 shift-workers, and about 20 shift-workers were employed at other textile factories where knitted garments, etc., were produced. The proportion which these shift women bore to the whole of the women employed is stated in the table, but the figures quoted are not always reliable. On an average, the shift women formed a third of the whole, but the proportion ranged between the extremes of 5 and 100 per cent.

Metal and Engineering Industries.—The metal and engineering industries probably employ the next largest number of shift-workers. At one works 100 women were employed in drawing strips of aluminium from casting furnaces, and in feeding and guiding machines which rolled out aluminium plates. At several tinplate works small numbers of women were engaged in slitting and opening tinplates. As there were not more than 25 at any one works they are not referred to in the table. At a wire manufacturer's some of the women, about 50 in all, were employed in setting up and tending wire-drawing machines, in which revolving rollers dragged the wire through a series of narrowing holes so as to reduce it to a thin gauge. Other women were employed in passing this wire through a bath of acid, and subsequently through a bath of molten zinc. At a factory devoted to electrical engineering about half of the 100 shift-workers were engaged in winding wire on wireless accumulator coils, while others were employed on lathes and riveting machines. At a factory devoted to general engineering the lathe-workers were engaged in turning and grinding large nuts and screws on hand-operated machines. At another engineering works—not recorded in the table—the monorail cranes were controlled by 28 two-shift women, for they were found to be more satisfactory at this type of work than men.

Miscellaneous Industries.—Of the other industries recorded in the table, a group of 250 women were engaged in weighing out sugar and packing it in 1-lb. packets, while at another factory 60 women were packing margarine. At three small factories groups of 20 to 30 women were engaged in packing yeast for use in bread-making. In each case they represented 80 to 100 per cent. of the women employed, so the figures have been combined in the table. At two factories groups of 270 and 80 women respectively were employed in the manufacture of rubber tyres. At a papermill 200 women were employed in tending machines which cut up cardboard and made it into boxes, while at a printing works 60 women were employed in tending machines which folded and stuck sheets of paper so as to form paper bags and cartons. At two other works groups of 120 and 60 women respectively were employed in rope-spinning and on parqueting machines, while at a candle factory 70 women were employed on doubling and braiding machines which manufactured candle-wicks.

The various industries and occupations mentioned represent only a fraction of those in which women have at one time or another been employed continuously on the two-shift system, but as a rule the numbers engaged were very small, not often exceeding 20. For instance, 16 women were employed at an enamelled-tile works, 15 at a wood flourmill, 18 at a brickworks, and 20 to 30 at each of three breweries. A number of other industries are referred to subsequently.

104 THE SHORTER WORKING WEEK

OUTPUT AND LOSS OF WORKING TIME

Persons employed on the two-shift system almost invariably work for fewer hours a day than those on the ordinary day-shift, and consequently their speed of production might be expected to be greater. The extent of this improvement—if it exists—cannot be predicted, so it must be ascertained by careful observation. It is by no means easy to obtain suitable data for the purpose, as it is necessary to find closely-comparable groups of workers employed at piece rates on occupations in which the rate of production can be accurately measured; or still better, to get the output of the same individuals when working for alternate periods of fairly considerable duration on shift-work and ordinary day-work. The two investigators of the Industrial Fatigue Research Board previously mentioned were fortunate in being able to obtain suitable data at five different factories, and their results are summarised in the table on page 105, which is taken from their Report.[1]

All of the women referred to in this table, except the lathe-workers (a) at Factory F, were originally on day-work and then changed over to shift-work, or *vice versa*. The lathe-workers in question comprised two parallel groups, each of five workers, one group being on day-work and the other on shift-work. The weekly hours of work recorded for the shift-workers are the averages of the 43 to 45 hours worked by the shifts in the morning and the $37\frac{1}{2}$ hours worked in the afternoon in alternate weeks.

Of the individual groups referred to, the 39 coil-winders at the electrical engineering Factory B are recorded as a whole and as a selected group (b) who were employed continuously throughout the experimental period on

---

[1] Smith, M. and Vernon, M.D., Report No. 47 of Indust. Fatigue Res. Board, 1928, p. 19

winding the same type of coil. Both this group of coil-winders and that at Factory E were engaged in winding wire on wireless accumulator coils, an occupation which is only semi-automatic as it requires considerable skill in guiding the wire. The output per hour is recorded in the table in relative terms, the average output of both shift-

COMPARISON OF OUTPUT ON DAY-WORK AND SHIFT-WORK

Factory.	Number of Workers.	Relative output per hour.			Hours of labour.		Relative output per week.	
		Shift-workers.	Day-workers.	Difference.	Shift-workers.	Day-workers.	Shift-workers.	Day-workers.
		%	%	%			%	%
B {	39 Coil-winders (a)	101	97	4	40¾	47	95	105
	7 Coil-winders (b)	102	95	7	40¾	47	97	103
E {	30 Coil-winders ...	100	100	0	40¾	47	93	107
	6 Engravers ...	104	97	7	40¾	47	96	104
D	18–30 Wire-drawers	99	101	−2	43½	47	95	105
F {	5 Lathe-workers (a)	111	90	21	41¼	{ 49 / 55 }	102 / 96	98 / 104
	9 Lathe-workers (b)	109	92	17	41¼	{ 49 / 55 }	100 / 94	100 / 106
G {	10 Cable-workers (a)	115	85	30	41¼	49	106	94
	10 Cable-workers (b)	111	89	22	41¼	49	102	98
	Average ...	106	94	12	41	49	98	102

workers and day-workers being taken as 100. It will be seen that at Factory B the hourly output of the coil-winders on shift-work was 4 to 7 per cent. greater than that of the day-workers, but at Factory E it was the same under the two systems of shift. This lack of improvement in the shift-workers may have been due to the fact that they were employed on shifts only for three months altogether, at a very hot time of the year, and it is possible that they never became sufficiently used to the change to reach their full output.

The output of the 18 to 30 wire-drawers employed at Factory D was 2 per cent. *less* when they were on shift-work than when on day-work, but this result is not very reliable, as the output was found to be very variable, and its measurement was subject to many unavoidable irregularities. All the other groups of workers investigated showed a substantially better output when they were on shift-work. The engravers at Factory E, who were engraving vulcanite plates with metal styles, showed a 7 per cent. excess on the day-shift output, while the lathe- and cable-workers at Factories F and G showed a 17 to 30 per cent. difference. The lathe-workers at Factory F were employed on the arduous work of turning and grinding large nuts and screws, while the cable-workers at Factory G were occupied on the light work of tending the machines which wound insulating paper round the wire cables, and joining the paper when it broke.

It will be seen that, on an average, the relative hourly output of the day-workers was 94, and as they put in 49 hours of work their weekly production rate came to 49×94, or to 4,606. The hourly output of the shift-workers averaged 106, and as they put in 41 hours of work their weekly production rate came to 4,346. This figure is 5·6 per cent. less than that of the day-workers, but the output of the two shifts, who together worked 82 hours per week, came to 88·7 per cent. *more* than that of the day-workers. Thus:

	Weekly hours of labour.	Hourly output.	Output per week.
Day-workers (1 shift)	49	94	$49 \times 94 = 4,606$ (=100)
Shift-workers (1 shift)	41	106	$41 \times 106 = 4,346$ (= 94·4)
Shift-workers (2 shifts)	82	106	$82 \times 106 = 8,692$ (=188·7)

TWO-SHIFT IN CONTINUOUS OPERATION

The hours worked are indicated diagrammatically in Fig. 7.

Loss of Working Time.—The greater speed of production of the shift-workers may have been due to their working faster, or to their losing less working time in the factory, or to both these causes combined. The loss of working

FIG. 7.—Comparison of hours worked under single-shift and two-shift systems.

time is partly involuntary and partly voluntary. The involuntary time is due to such causes as fetching and carrying material, and getting the machines adjusted, while the voluntary time is due to the operatives stopping work of their own volition in order to talk or rest. In several factories an attempt was made to compare the times lost in these ways by shift-workers and day-workers engaged on the same or similar types of work, and the table indicates the results obtained with the most closely comparable groups:

	Shift-workers.			Day-workers.			
	Minutes per hour lost.				Minutes per hour lost.		
	Involuntarily.	Voluntarily.	Total.		Involuntarily.	Voluntarily.	Total.
6 art. silk-winders	2·2	0·7	2·9	6 art. silk-winders	3·3	3·2	6·6
6 coil-winders ...	1·1	1·9	3·0	5 coil-winders ...	2·1	8·7	10·8
6 lathe-workers ...	2·3	9·7	12·0	6 lathe-workers ...	3·9	8·3	12·2
Average ...	1·9	4·1	6·0		3·1	6·8	9·9

It will be seen that, on an average, the day-workers lost distinctly more time than the shift-workers, both from involuntary and voluntary causes. Altogether they lost 9·9 minutes per hour, so it follows that they worked for 50·1 minutes in each hour. The shift-workers lost 6·0 minutes per hour, and therefore worked for 54·0 minutes. This working time is 8 per cent. greater than that of the day-workers, while the hourly rate of production recorded in the previous table showed an improvement of 13 per cent. As the groups of workers included in the two tables are to a large extent different, it is not possible to make a close comparison between them, but the data suggest that the shift-workers owe their greater hourly output more or less equally to losing less working time and to accelerating their speed of actual working.

It was found that the afternoon shift lost more time, both voluntarily and involuntarily, than the morning shift, the total times for the two shifts averaging 4·0 and 6·5 minutes respectively in the groups of workers compared. The time lost increased gradually and fairly steadily throughout the day, and it was interesting to note that it was no greater between the hours of 6 to 8 a.m. and 7 to 10 p.m., when the shift-workers were labouring alone and the supervision may have been inadequate, than from 8 a.m. to 7 p.m., when they were labouring in company with the day-workers.

Time-keeping.—At some factories complaints have been made of the bad time-keeping of the shift-workers. It was said that the morning shift were liable to come late, while the workers on the afternoon shift occasionally asked permission to leave at 8 p.m., apparently in order to visit places of amusement. Some statistical evidence of time-keeping was obtained[1] at two factories, and it gave some support to these complaints, though it was not very substantial. At the large artificial silk factory

[1] Smith and Vernon, *l.c.*, p. 25.

previously mentioned, data relating to 76 day-workers and 188 shift-workers were obtained over a period of two years. On an average the day-workers lost 2·0 hours per worker per week, or 4·4 per cent. of their nominal hours of work, while the shift-workers lost 2·6 hours, or 6·5 per cent. of their hours. On the other hand, at the electrical engineering factory previously mentioned there were 6 per cent. more cases of lateness among the day-workers than among the shift-workers. Their lateness was less serious, however, for the day-workers rarely lost more than a quarter to half an hour, while about a tenth of the shift-workers, when they were late, arrived at 8 a.m. along with the day-workers, instead of at 6 a.m.

In some instances the bad time-keeping of the morning shift was almost unavoidable, as it was due to the difficulties of transport. Some firms recognised this fact, and either acquiesced in the late arrivals, or did their best to arrange for better transport facilities.

THE DEPENDENCE OF RATE OF PRODUCTION ON HOURS OF WORK

The increase of production rate observed when the hours of work were reduced from 49 to 41 a week cannot be held to apply to industry in general. No hard and fast rule can be laid down as to the improvement to be expected if a two-shift system, with its shortened hours, were widely adopted in place of the present one-shift system, for the effect produced varies so greatly with the type of work concerned. A considerable amount of investigation on the effect of reducing hours of work has been made for many years past, and it is worth while to describe some of it briefly, as it will help to indicate the principle on which the degree of improvement depends. It will be simplest to describe first some results which were obtained in munition works during the war,[1] as they illustrate it very closely.

At a factory where about 10,000 workers were mostly engaged in making time-fuses, the nominal hours of work were at first 12 a day on Monday to Friday, and shorter hours on Saturday and Sunday. The total hours came to $74\frac{1}{2}$ a week, on an average, but owing to sickness the time-keeping was so bad that the actual hours worked were considerably less. After a time the workers were put on to a 10-hour day, and their hours then averaged $63\frac{1}{2}$ a week. Later on, Sunday labour was abolished and the hours fell to $55\frac{1}{2}$ a week, so there were three clear-cut systems of hours during which output could be ascertained. The output of a group of 66 to 100 women engaged in turning aluminium fuse bodies on capstan lathes was investigated over a period of 93 consecutive weeks, and it was found that while at first, during the period of very long hours, the articles were produced at a (relative) rate of 108 per hour, this rate increased to 131 per hour in the second period, and to 169 per hour in the third period. The actual hours worked in the three periods averaged 66·0, 54·4 and 47·5 per week respectively, so the total weekly output varied in the following manner:

In the 74·5-hour week total output was 66·0 × 108
$$= 7,128 (= 100)$$
,, ,, 63·5 ,, ,, ,, ,, ,, 54·4 × 131
$$= 7,126 (= 100)$$
,, ,, 55·5 ,, ,, ,, ,, ,, 47·5 × 169
$$= 8,028 (= 113).$$

It will be seen that a reduction in the nominal hours of work of 19 per week, and in the actual hours of $18\frac{1}{2}$ per week, led to an increase of 13 per cent. in the total pro-

[1] Vernon, H. M., *cf.* Memos. Nos. 12 and 18 of Health of Munition Workers Committee, 1916 and 1917; *also* Report No. 6 of Indust. Fatigue Res. Board, 1920.

duction. This was due to the increased hourly rate of production consequent on the diminution of fatigue, for there was no change whatever in the character of the occupation.

Other munition-workers studied included a group of 27 to 90 men who were employed on the strenuous occupation of sizing fuse bodies. This was entirely hand-work, as the men had merely to fasten each fuse body to a handle and screw it rapidly into a steel tap. The hourly rate of production of the men was found to be 37 per cent. greater when they were on a $55\frac{1}{2}$-hour week than when on one of 66·7 hours, and their weekly productivity was 19 per cent. greater. The more marked improvement observed in these men than in the women turning fuse bodies was due to the fact that they could accelerate their speed of work without any limit at every stage of their job, while the women were to some extent limited by the mechanical conditions under which they worked. Another group of women, who were engaged in milling a screw thread on the fuse bodies, were still more limited by the machinery as it was semi-automatic, and though they increased their hourly rate of production 33 per cent. when they changed from a 71·8-hour week to one of 57·3 hours, their weekly output fell 1 per cent. Finally a group of youths engaged in boring "top caps," an operation absolutely limited in speed by the machine, were found to increase their hourly rate of production 21 per cent. when they changed from a 76·8-hour week to one of 60·1 hours, but the reduction of working hours was so considerable that the increased hourly rate of production could not compensate for it, and the weekly output fell 7 per cent.

These munition factory data, therefore, indicate clearly that the improvement of output induced by shortening the hours of work depends on the extent to which the occupation is dependent on machinery and on hand-work. If it is dependent entirely on automatic machinery the output can be improved only by greater promptness in starting up the machinery at the beginning of the work spells, in reducing the delays caused by breakdowns and readjustments, and so on ; but the more the occupation is dependent on the human element and the less on the mechanical element the greater are the possibilities of improvement in the actual speed of production. There must naturally be some limit to this improvement, and the hours of work cannot be reduced beyond a certain point if output is to be maintained. What this limit is we do not know at all definitely, but a certain amount of information on the subject has been obtained in a number of industries.[1] They may conveniently be classified in three groups, according to the degree of dependence on the human element.

(a) *Industries dependent chiefly on Handwork.*—The most important industry coming under this category is coal-mining, for in this country the larger part of the coal is cut by hand, and not by machinery. No accurate statistics are available of the effects of reducing working hours from 8 to 7 in 1919, and of the subsequent return to the longer working day in 1926, but in America (Illinois) it was found that the output during 1898–1900, when an 8-hour day was worked, was 19 per cent. greater than in 1894–96, when a 10-hour day was worked. The proportion of coal cut by machinery was about 20 per cent. in both periods, and the improvement was ascribed to the increased energy and promptness of the men.

In the industry of granite-cutting, which is dependent chiefly on hand labour, it was found by a firm in America that under identically the same conditions the men attained a bigger output when on a working day of 9 hours than on one of 10 hours, and a considerably bigger output when on one of 8 hours. It was thought probable that as

[1] For detailed information *cf.* H. M. Vernon, *Industrial Efficiency and Fatigue*, London, 1921, pp. 62–76.

good an output would have been attained on a 7-hour day, but the surmise was not put to a practical test.

(b) *Industries dependent more or less equally on Handwork and on Machinery.*—A classical example of the effects of shortening hours of work in this type of labour was afforded by Abbé. At the Zeiss works, Jena, twelve groups of men engaged on various occupations connected with the production of optical instruments had their hours of work reduced from 9 to 8 a day, and every group showed a substantial increase in their hourly rate of production. It varied from 9 to 20 per cent., and the weekly production of the 233 men concerned showed an average increase of 3·3 per cent.

At two engineering works in England it was found that production was slightly greater when the men were on a 48-hour week than when on one of 54 hours, while output was fully maintained at a large number of Government factories and ordnance works when the hours were similarly reduced. Over 60,000 men were affected by this change, and it was found, not only that the men on piece-work earned as much as before, but that those on a time rate likewise maintained their output.

(c) *Industries dependent chiefly on Machinery.*—The most important industries falling in this class are the textile industries. The majority of the processes involved are dependent to an outstanding degree on machinery; *e.g.*, in spinning a single operative may tend as many as 1,000 spindles. The spinner has to join together the ends of any yarns which become broken, but the average loss of time from breakage of yarn is said to represent less than 1 per cent. of the total spindle time. Employers generally maintain that a reduction of hours of work, *e.g.*, from 55 to 49½ a week, leads to a proportionate reduction of output, but at some factories it has been found that it is proportionate to about half the reduction of hours. However, the output per spindle and per loom in Massachusetts was found to be as great on a 10-hour day as on one of 11 hours.

In wool manufacture it was found, in America, that a reduction of hours from 57 to 54 a week almost always resulted in a decreased output, but in silk manufacture the effects were rather more favourable. When the hours were reduced from 55 or 52 to 50 a week, output was improved in 2 of the 58 factories investigated and maintained in 9 of them. In 19 factories there was a loss of output proportional to the reduction of hours, and in 23, to one somewhat less than proportional.

In weaving, the human element plays a larger part than in spinning, and it is probable that maximum output is attained on an $8\frac{1}{2}$- or 9-hour day.

The information summarised above, though very imperfect, is sufficient to indicate that no hard-and-fast rule can be laid down as to the effect of the adoption of the two-shift system on the speed of production in various industries. It seems probable, however, that in occupations dependent wholly or chiefly on handwork, the speed of production would be so much increased when a 41-hour week was substituted for a 47-hour week that the output would fall off little if at all. On the other hand, in industries dependent chiefly on machinery the output would undoubtedly fall off, and in some of them the reduction might be almost proportionate to the reduction of hours. Taking industry as a whole, it seems probable that the speed of production would be accelerated by something like 10 per cent. when the shorter shifts were adopted. That is to say, the total weekly production on the 41-hour week would come to $41 \times 110 = 4,510$, as compared with one of $47 \times 100 = 4,700$ on the 47-hour week. This means a reduction of 4 per cent. for each of the two shifts, but an increase of 92 per cent. for the two shifts combined.

THE WAGES PAID

The success of the two-shift system is probably bound up more closely with the question of wages than with any other factor. If the workers, when on shift-work, are paid as much as when they were previously on day-work, they almost always acquiesce in the system or accept it with approval; but if their wages are reduced, and especially if they are reduced proportionately to the shorter hours worked, the system meets with their uncompromising opposition. On several occasions the inspectors reported that the workers were reluctant to sanction the adoption of the system as they feared its effects on wages.

Though no statistical evidence is available, it appears that the majority of the employers fully realise the importance of the wage question, and pay the shift-workers, when on day rates, as much as they formerly received when on ordinary day shift, while they raise the rate of pay of the piece-workers to such a figure that they are able to earn as much, or nearly as much, as before. From the information adduced in the previous section, it will be realised that it may be impossible to fix a piece rate which yields exactly the same weekly wage as before, so it must sometimes happen that the weekly wage is slightly reduced, while in other cases it is slightly increased. It is stated that in some instances the firms found that they did not need to raise the piece rate at all, as the workers were able to compensate for the shorter hours by their increased speed of production, but I have not been able to obtain any details of these cases.

At a few factories the shift-workers appear to have been definitely paid higher wages than the day-workers. Thus, at a factory where over a fourth of the 1,000 women employed in manufacturing hosiery were on shifts, and where in consequence they worked only $7\frac{1}{2}$ hours a day as against the 8¾ hours of the day women, the hourly rate of pay was raised 20 per cent. This meant a 3 per cent. higher wage than that of the day women. At another factory, where the same wages were paid to shift-workers and day-workers, the regulations—which do not allow shift-work for young persons under 16—led to a most contradictory arrangement of hours. The young girls coming fresh to the factory at the age of 14 had to work a 10-hour day (viz., from 6 a.m. to 5.30 p.m.) until they attained the age of 16, and then they were put on to the 7½-hour day worked by the older girls and the women. Naturally the girls were glad to reach the age when they were transferred to shift-work; but at an adjoining factory the shift-workers were not paid sufficiently to compensate for the shorter hours, so the system was very unpopular. This unpopularity was to some extent overcome by putting all the freshly-engaged girls—if over 16—on shift-work at first, and transferring them to day-work after three months.

The payment of the same wages to the shift-workers as to the day-workers was found, in one or two instances, to cause discontent among the latter, but it is obvious that no conceivable system of payment would appear strictly equitable to both classes of workers.

Of the various factories where the same hourly rate was paid to shift-workers as to day-workers, it was reported that at one factory the employees were "emphatically in favour of day-work." At another factory the shift-workers "envied the day-workers who worked 9½ or 10½ hours a day," as they could earn so much more. The hardest case of all was met with at a factory where the shift-workers were allowed 1 hour for meals instead of the usual ½-hour. Consequently they worked only 7 hours per shift, and as the hourly rate of pay was very low in the industry in question, the complaints were very bitter.

THE INFLUENCE OF THE TWO-SHIFT SYSTEM ON HEALTH

Whatever the immediate advantage of the two-shift system to production, it will be generally admitted that its ultimate value depends largely upon its influence on the health of the workers. If this influence is adverse, no addition of output can be held to compensate for the damage done to the women and girls who in the great majority of cases spend only a few years at factory life, and then settle down, as married women, to manage a household and bear offspring. Great attention has, therefore, been paid to the subject of health, both by the welfare supervisors at the factories where the system is installed, and by the Factory Inspectors who have made it their object to pay frequent visits to these factories. The evidence is naturally somewhat conflicting, but the weight of opinion in favour of the system appears to outweigh that against it. This conclusion is in fair agreement with the statistical evidence collected by the investigators of the Industrial Fatigue Research Board.

Statistical Evidence of Sickness.—At the artificial silk factory previously mentioned, careful records were kept of the attendance of the workers at the first-aid station.[1] The number of visits paid on full working days (Monday to Friday) by 1,400 to 2,000 workers was ascertained for a year, and the visits were tabulated in three groups for (*a*) departments always on shift-work, (*b*) departments always on day-work, and (*c*) departments changing from shift-work to day-work, or *vice versa*, during the year. Secondly, all the departments were taken month by month and grouped according to whether the workers were on shift-work or day-work at the time. The average numbers of visits paid per 100 workers per annum are recorded in the table on page 118.

It will be seen that distinctly more accidents were

[1] *L.c.* p. 26.

incurred by shift-workers than by day-workers. This was because more of the former group were employed on machines—where it was easy to incur accidents—than of the latter. Ignoring these cases, the visits due to sickness

NUMBER OF VISITS TO FIRST-AID STATION PER 100 WORKERS PER ANNUM

	Causes of visits.						Total omitting accidents.
	Accidents.	Respiratory diseases.	Headache and neuralgia.	Faintness and dizziness.	Disorders of digestive system.	Other causes.	
Depts. always on shift-work	42	13	26	9	14	39	101
Depts. always on day-work	30	11	25	6	9	50	101
Depts. changing from shift-work to day-work or vice versa	38	13	29	10	10	40	102
Difference between depts. on shift-work and day-work	12	2	1	3	5	−11	0
All shift-workers	42	13	26	9	13	42	103
All day-workers	29	11	24	7	10	40	92
Difference	13	2	2	2	3	2	11

were exactly the same in number from departments always on shift-work and those always on day-work; but when the workers were classified according to the character of their work at the time, a slight excess of sickness showed itself among the shift-workers. Taking the data as a whole, it may be said that the shift-workers probably tended to suffer slightly more from faintness and disorders of the digestive system than the day-workers, but owing to the large monthly variations in the number of cases the difference was not great enough to be significant in the statistical sense.

The Evidence of Welfare Supervisors and Inspectors.—The evidence of the welfare supervisors at the factories where the two-shift system was installed, and of the inspectors who visited them, is for the most part based on general impressions. It may, therefore, be subject to unconscious bias, the result of preconceived opinions; but if taken on a fairly large scale it is undoubtedly of value. The evidence obtained may conveniently be classified under the three headings (1) favourable, (2) neutral (*i.e.*, showing a rough balance between favourable and unfavourable), and (3) unfavourable.

(1) *Favourable Evidence.*

(*a*) All the welfare supervisors interrogated asserted that they had found no ill-effects from shift-work, even when continued over a long period.

(*b*) At a tin-box factory employing 250 shift-workers, the absenteeism over a three-month period was considerably less in the shift-workers than in the others.

(*c*) No evidence was obtained that the changing mealtimes caused by shifts upset digestion, or disorganised home life.

(*d*) The supervisors at two works said that in their experience the health of the women, as indicated by timekeeping and absenteeism, was better on shift-work than on day-work.

(*e*) In two cases the managers administering the funds of " sick clubs " at the works, stated that their payments to shift-workers were less than to day-workers.

(*f*) The supervisor said that the girls were definitely

fresher under the two-shift system than after working long days which included overtime.

(g) The health of the shift women is good, and absenteeism negligible.

(2) *Neutral Evidence.*

(a) There is very little evidence of any effect on health. Some of the women say that they do not eat so well when on shifts, and miss an hour of sleep; many of them have to do more housework, but on the other hand, they get the benefit of more fresh air and sunshine, and more opportunity of playing outdoor games.

(b) A foreman at one factory said that the workers on the afternoon shift seemed tired, but a foreman at another factory found the shift girls to be fresher than the others.

(3) *Unfavourable Evidence.*

(a) One or two welfare supervisors stated that they had several cases of faintness as a result of a long walk to the works by the early shift-workers without a proper meal before starting. Some of the shift-workers complained of the change of meal-times, and some of them had done so much housework at home in the mornings that they were tired when they got to the factory for the afternoon shift.

(b) A nurse at a welfare department had observed cases of faintness due to the women taking no food before work on the morning shift.

(c) A few workers said that the early-morning rising gave them a headache; others could not eat before work; others objected to the variable meal-times, and others to loss of sleep, but no evidence was obtainable pointing to an ill-effect on health.

(d) The supervisors thought that the shift-work must be bad for health, but they had no figures to support their impressions.

(e) The supervisors said that shift-work was bad for

health, but they could not substantiate their view by precise data.

(f) A nurse said that the girls' health suffered; they were more tired than after ordinary day-work.

(g) The girls said that "they do not feel nearly so well when at shifts."

It will probably be agreed that this evidence, taken as a whole, is more in favour of the two-shift system than against it, but it clearly raises several points which require further elucidation. The most important of these relate to the effects of the shift system on home life, more especially in relation to hours of sleep, housework, and meals. Some information on the subject was given by the Industrial Fatigue Board investigators in their report,[1] and they have been good enough to provide me with the detailed statistics upon which it was founded. Some of this evidence I am quoting in the course of the next few pages.

The Hours of Sleep.—At several factories some of the women were questioned orally, one at a time, about their customary habits of sleep, meals, and housework. At Factories A (artificial silk), B (electrical engineering), C (paper-bag manufacture), and D (wire manufacture) more than 200 women were questioned in all, and the answers obtained from the women on morning shift concerning their times of going to bed and getting up are summarised in the table in the form of percentages.

HOURS OF SLEEP OF MORNING SHIFT

Per cent. of workers getting up:	Per cent. of workers going to bed:	Per cent. of workers spending in bed:
Before 4.30 a.m. ... 11	Before 10 p.m. ... 38	Under 7 hours ... 55
4.30 to 5.30 a.m. ... 72	10 to 11 p.m. ... 54	7 to 8 hours ... 40
After 5.30 a.m. ... 17	After 11 p.m. ... 8	8 to 9 hours ... 5

[1] *L.c.* p. 28.

It will be seen that the majority of the workers, when on morning shift, went to bed some time between 10 and 11 p.m., and got up at some time between 4.30 and 5.30 a.m. In consequence, over half of them got less than 7 hours' sleep, and only 5 per cent. of them got over 8 hours. In order to indicate more exactly the most usual hours of sleep, the *median* times at the four factories are recorded in the next table. A median time affords a

MEDIAN HOURS OF SLEEP OF MORNING SHIFT

	Factories starting work at 6 a.m.			Factory starting at 6.30.
	A	B	D	C
Median time of getting up	4.45 a.m.	4.47 a.m.	5.7 a.m.	5.33 a.m.
Median time of going to bed	9.57 p.m.	10.39 p.m.	9.57 p.m.	10.0 p.m.
Median number of hours of sleep	$6\frac{3}{4}$	$6\frac{1}{2}$	$6\frac{3}{4}$	$7\frac{1}{2}$
Number of workers questioned	90	50	23	40

better measure than an average time, which is unduly influenced by extreme values in either direction, for it shows such a time that half of all the ascertained values fall below it in magnitude, and half above it. We see that this median time ranged from $6\frac{1}{2}$ to $6\frac{3}{4}$ hours at Factories A, B and D, which started work at 6 a.m., but it amounted to $7\frac{1}{2}$ hours at Factory C, which did not start till 6.30 a.m. The data are not sufficiently numerous to warrant definite conclusions, but it certainly appears that most of the women had the habit of going to bed at about 10 p.m., whatever time they had to get up in the morning. Probably it was almost impossible for most of them to go to bed much earlier, because of the crowded houses and noisy districts in which they lived; but many of them got an additional rest by lying down in the afternoons, after they returned from work. This is indicated by the following data:

	Factory A.	Factory B.	Factory D.	Mean.
Per cent. of workers lying down regularly in the afternoons ...	27	37	39	34
Per cent. of workers lying down occasionally in the afternoons	36	52	30	39
Per cent. of workers never lying down	36	11	30	26

The women said that they lay down for a period of 1 to 4 hours, so that the great majority of them must have obtained sufficient rest in spite of their somewhat reduced hours of sleep at night. If they did not do so, it must often have been their own fault for not making a custom of lying down regularly in the afternoons.

The afternoon shift-workers naturally got up much later than those on morning shift, and it was found that, on an average, 25 per cent. of them got up before 9 a.m., 50 per cent. between 9 and 10 a.m., and 25 per cent. after 10 a.m. For the workers at Factories A, B and D the median time of getting up varied from 9.20 to 9.50 a.m., but for those at Factory C (where the afternoon shift stopped work at 8 p.m.) it was 9.0 a.m. It seems to follow that the shift-workers, if they did not obtain sufficient sleep during their morning shift weeks, were able to make up for the deficiency by getting extra sleep in the alternating afternoon shift weeks.

Meals before Work.—It will have been noted that a few welfare supervisors reported cases of faintness among the women coming on to work at 6 a.m., but it seems probable that such cases were not specially due to the early rising. On tabulating all the cases of faintness treated during a period of a year at the first-aid station at the large artificial silk factory previously mentioned, it was found that between the hours of 6 and 8 a.m. the faintness cases occurred at the rate of 1·0 per cent. per hour (calculated on all the sickness cases per shift). Between 8 and 10 a.m., when the shift-workers in question were augmented by a nearly equal number of ordinary day-workers, the faintness figures for the whole body of women still averaged 1·0 per cent., but between 10 a.m. and 12 noon they fell to 0·6 per cent. Between 1 and 5 p.m. they averaged 0·9 per cent., while from 7 to 10 p.m., when the day-workers had departed and the shift-workers were working alone, they rose to 1·5 per cent. These data, so far as they go, seem to indicate that the shift system tended to induce an increase of faintness in the second-shift women when they were working alone in the evening, but this conclusion is very doubtful. At some factories it was found that a few of the women, when working by themselves in the evening, got so bored that at times they seized on almost any excuse for getting away from the factory. A slight feeling of dizziness might easily be magnified to serve their purpose.

Quite apart from the possibility that lack of food may induce faintness, it is important that the workers should have a meal of some sort before coming on to work, for it will be remembered that, in accordance with the regulations, they are unable to take their half-hour meal break till 8.30 a.m. at the earliest, and generally it is postponed till 9.0 or 9.30 a.m. The workers at the four factories previously mentioned were questioned individually about their meals, and the information obtained is recorded statistically in the table.

BREAKFAST TAKEN BY MORNING SHIFT

	Factories starting at 6 a.m.				Factory starting at 6.30 a.m.
	A.	B.	D.	Mean.	
Per cent. of workers having proper breakfast	62	26	41	43	90
Per cent. of workers having tea and a little food	17	40	18	25	10
Per cent. of workers having tea only	19	26	32	26	0
Per cent. of workers having nothing...	2	8	9	6	0

It will be seen that, on an average, at the three factories where the morning shift started at 6 a.m., 43 per cent. of the women had a proper breakfast before they went to work, while another 25 per cent. of them had tea and a little food. Of the remainder, 26 per cent. had tea only, and 6 per cent. nothing at all. The preparation of a proper breakfast takes time, and for this reason some of the women may have omitted it, but any woman who took the trouble to make tea could easily have eaten some food (*e.g.*, bread and butter or biscuits) with very little expenditure of extra time if she had an inclination to do so. Some of the women said that they had no appetite for food at the early hour, and though such disinclination may be fairly common among industrial workers when they first start work at 6 a.m., they can gradually acquire the habit of eating a good meal if they persist in the effort.

It will be observed that at Factory C, which did not start till 6.30 a.m., almost the whole of the 40 workers questioned had a proper breakfast before work. Probably this was due largely to their living near the factory, for only four of them took more than 20 minutes to get there from their homes.

The Duration of the Meal Break.—The duration of the meal break under the two-shift system is almost always half an hour. Some authorities maintain that this is not long enough for eating and digesting a substantial meal, and on the Continent a working day with a meal break of not more than half an hour is termed an " unbroken " working day.[1] Certainly half an hour is much too short if the workers have to go home for their meal, but such an arrangement is wholly exceptional, and is followed only in a few instances where the workers live close to the factory. They almost always have their food in a messroom in the factory itself, and half an hour is probably sufficient for this purpose in most instances. Coal-miners, who have to perform far more strenuous work than almost any shift-workers, get a " snap time " of only 20 to 30 minutes, but this brief interval does not seem to harm their digestion. If further investigation suggests that the half-hour is too short for the shift-workers, it could easily be lengthened to 40, 50 or 60 minutes.

Housework.—Shift-workers sometimes complain that when they are on the afternoon shift they are tired before they start factory work, as they have had to do so much housework at home in the morning. The possibility of doing housework is considered by many married women to be one of the chief advantages of the two-shift system, as they are able to look after their homes and their children during a part of the day ; but the unmarried women, especially if young, are naturally inclined to regard it as drudgery to which they ought not to be subjected. The results of questioning the workers at the factories previously referred to are indicated in the table on page 127.

It will be seen that about a third of the women did a regular and substantial amount of housework. Another

---

[1] Milhaud, M., *Internat. Lab. Rev.* 26, p. 797, 1932.

third did it occasionally, or regularly but in small amount, while the remainder did none. The women who said that they did occasional housework or regular housework in small amount, appeared to do odd jobs such as washing-up, shopping, etc., and these were probably not sufficient to tire them and reduce their efficiency; but regular and

HOUSEWORK DONE BY SHIFT-WORKERS

	Factories starting at 6 a.m.			
	A.	B.	D.	Mean.
Per cent. of workers doing housework regularly	39	34	30	34
Per cent. of workers doing housework occasionally	28	38	50	39
Per cent. of workers doing no housework ...	33	28	20	27

substantial housework is undoubtedly a considerable hardship for women who are doing active work at the factory. If they are engaged on light sedentary work they may not get unduly fatigued by their double tasks, and a certain amount of standing or walking about at home may be good for them, but it will be generally admitted that in these days of mechanical production $7\frac{1}{2}$ hours of factory work a day ought to earn immunity from any but very light housework.

THE INFLUENCE OF THE THREE-SHIFT SYSTEM ON HEALTH

Some light upon the influence of the two-shift system on health, especially in so far as it may upset digestion and induce fatigue owing to deficient sleep, is afforded by studying the effects of the more exacting three-shift system. This system is followed by hundreds of thousands of men who habitually work in certain continuous occupations such as are met with in many branches of the iron and steel trades, in glass manufacture, and other industries. These men usually work in three 8-hour shifts, which run from 6 a.m. to 2 p.m., 2 to 10 p.m., and 10 p.m. to 6 a.m. They change shifts every week, so they have to work on night shift every third week. In most occupations work stops at 2 p.m. on Saturdays, and does not start again till Sunday night or Monday morning, so the men have their week-end free, but in a few of them—*e.g.*, the smelting of iron in blast furnaces—the work is continuous the whole year round, and the men have to work over the week-ends.

Many of the iron and steel men have to perform very heavy work, and they are often exposed to very high temperatures. Hence they are specially liable to catch chills and get pneumonia, bronchitis, and other diseases of the respiratory system. Also they lose a good deal of time from injuries and from rheumatism. Nevertheless their sickness rate, taken as a whole, is not excessive, and is not much greater than that of men employed in other industries on day work only, under ordinary temperature conditions. An investigation of the sickness data of 22,000 iron and steel workers (aged 16 to 70) for the years 1913–18[1] showed an average loss of 6·5 working days per year by the whole body of men. The men on very hot and heavy work lost 7·7 days, and those on light work at ordinary temperatures, 6·0 days. These figures are not much in excess of those observed in a sample of the whole insured population for the years 1921–23,[2] where the sickness rate ranged from 4·7 days per year for men aged 20–29 to 5·9 days for those aged 40–49 and 11·3 days for those aged 55 to 64.

[1] Vernon, H. M., and Rusher, E. A., Report No. 5 of Indust. Fatigue Res. Board, 1920.
[2] *Cf.* Hill, A. B., Report No. 54 of Indust. Fatigue Res. Board, 1929.

The mortality rate of the group of iron and steel-workers investigated was found to be slightly less than that of " all males, occupied and retired," recorded by the Registrar-General in the period 1910–12, but as the total deaths numbered only 310, it is better to rely on the more recent figures recorded by the Registrar-General for the years 1921–23.[1] The total deaths in the group of " persons engaged in smelting, rolling, converting of iron and steel " then numbered 3,204, and it will be seen from the table that the comparative mortality figure (between the

COMPARATIVE MORTALITY RATES OF MALES, AGED 20–65, IN 1921–23

Occupational group.	Comparative mortality from				
	All causes.	Diseases of respiratory system.	Diseases of digestive system.	Diseases of circulatory system.	Accidents.
All occupied and retired civilian males	1,000	152	60	152	49
Persons engaged in smelting, rolling, converting iron and steel	1,025	219	53	129	61
Puddlers	1,250	319	55	118	30
Skilled glasshouse workers	1,244	242	42	174	21
Coal-miners	1,034	187	51	147	117
Boilermakers and platers, and their labourers	968	155	67	149	45
Riveters and their labourers	1,062	201	47	149	58
Agricultural labourers	688	90	40	102	45

ages of 20 and 65) was only slightly greater than that of " all occupied and retired civilian males." But for the excessive mortality from respiratory diseases it would

[1] The Registrar-General's Decennial Supplement, 1921, Part II, Occupational Mortality, 1927.

have been distinctly lower than that of "all males." The group of "puddlers" is a better one for comparison purposes as it is homogeneous, instead of being a conglomeration of men employed in a number of very different occupations. The puddlers make wrought-iron in small puddling furnaces under very hot and arduous conditions, but the work is intermittent. They usually work very hard for about 20 minutes at a time and in consequence stream with perspiration. During the subsequent rest they are apt to catch a chill, so they are specially liable to pneumonia and other respiratory diseases. It will be seen that their mortality from these causes was double that of "all males," while the mortality of the "skilled glasshouse workers" (who manipulate molten glass) was likewise considerable. Yet all these groups of men, though working on the three-shift system throughout their industrial lives, had a distinctly lower mortality from diseases of the digestive system than the average. Hence the weekly change of meal-times did not appear to upset them, so far as these mortality figures offer a criterion.

A few other groups of industrial workers are introduced in the table for purposes of comparison. The majority of coal-miners work single day shifts, though in some coal-fields there are two day shifts, and in all of them there is a small permanent night shift of men on repair work. The groups of platers and riveters work only on day shift, and it will be seen that their mortality figures are similar to those of the group of men engaged in iron and steel production. Finally the group of agricultural labourers is quoted, for though they are the worst-paid of all industrial workers, they are the healthiest, owing to their open-air life. Their mortality from each of the causes stated in the table—except accidents—is only about two-thirds as great as that of "all males."

Though the evidence is not conclusive, we see that neither the sickness nor the mortality data indicate that the three-shift system, with its night shift in every third week, acts adversely on the health of the men who experience it. It would, therefore, be very unlikely that a two-shift system, which avoided the night shift completely, would have any adverse effect whatever.

CHAPTER VI

THE TWO-SHIFT SYSTEM IN INTERMITTENT OPERATION

CONTENTS

Seasonal Employment—Intermittent Employment not Related to Season—The Administration of Orders used Intermittently—The Occupations for which Orders have been Obtained—The Two-Shift System in Other Countries—The Employment of Boys on the Two-Shift System—Lighting, Heating and Ventilation under the Two-Shift System

SEASONAL EMPLOYMENT

It has already been pointed out that the two-shift system may be very useful in seasonal trades where there is a largely-increased demand during certain months of the year. As far as I can ascertain, the number of factories in which the system is used seasonally on a substantial scale is not large. The accompanying table indicates the

WOMEN EMPLOYED SEASONALLY UNDER THE TWO-SHIFT SYSTEM

Trade or Occupation.		Number of women on two-shift system.	Per cent. on total employed.
Production of food, etc.	Fruit-canning	90	22
	Fruit-canning	40	25
	Chocolates and Easter eggs	150	7
	Sugar-packing	75	10
	Beer-bottling	75	20
Miscellaneous industries	Wireless magnetos	40	(4)
	Nuts and bolts	30	(2)
	Moulding golf balls	200	(5)

eight factories known to me where 30 or more women were employed on seasonal trades in 1928, and probably there were about the same number of other factories which are not included.

Two fruit-canning factories are recorded in the table, and as the food-canning industry has developed so rapidly in the last few years, it is probable that at the present time a good many other factories have made use of the system. Thus it is stated[1] that the fruit and vegetable-canning industry " has especially benefited by being able to work shifts." The rush generally lasts for the four summer months, June to September. The seasonal rushes at chocolate factories are generally not so prolonged, as they usually last only a few weeks before Easter, when Easter eggs are manufactured, and for a few weeks before Christmas. The seasonal rush of sugar-packing is in the summer; that of beer-bottling is likewise in the summer, the rush being dependent to some extent on the advent of hot weather.

Of the miscellaneous trades, wireless magnetos are in increased demand during the winter months. The percentages of two-shift women quoted in the last column of the table for this and the other two miscellaneous trades are based on the total number of employees of both sexes, whilst those quoted for the food production trades represent the percentages on the number of women employed.

Other industries which sometimes employ two-shift workers seasonally are the ice-cream and wafer-biscuit industries, and biscuit manufacture in general. Again, the tin-canister factories which work in association with the fruit-canning factories experience a seasonal rush just as they do.

The Prevention of Overtime Work.—One of the greatest merits of the two-shift system is its prevention of overtime

---

[1] *Report of Chief Inspector of Factories for* 1931, p. 54.

work. Under existing Factory Acts[1] the overtime which may be worked under some circumstances is so excessive that it must cause undue fatigue and, in some cases, actual ill-health to the women involved. This undue fatigue is—or should be—entirely prevented by the two-shift system where, as we have seen, the hours of work do not exceed $7\frac{1}{2}$ a day. Under the Factory and Workshops Act of 1901, women aged 18 and upwards, and young persons of both sexes between 14 and 18, if employed in non-textile factories, may work from 6 a.m. to 6 p.m., 7 a.m. to 7 p.m., or 8 a.m. to 8 p.m., except on Saturday. As $1\frac{1}{2}$ hours are allowed for meals this means that $10\frac{1}{2}$ hours are worked per day. On Saturday the hours run from 6 a.m. to 2 p.m., 7 a.m. to 3 p.m., or 8 a.m. to 4 p.m., with at least half an hour off for a meal, so they amount to a maximum of $7\frac{1}{2}$ hours; but the total weekly hours of work must not exceed 60 hours, unless so-called "overtime" is worked. With a few strictly-limited exceptions, boys and girls under 18 may not be employed on overtime, but women may work for two hours extra (including half an hour for a meal) on three days a week for not more than 30 days a year in most industries. That is to say, their hours of work may extend over a period of 14 hours (*e.g.*, from 6 a.m. to 8 p.m.), and they may perform 12 hours of actual work on each of the three days. Their total hours, therefore, come to $64\frac{1}{2}$ per week. Women who are employed in preserving fruit and curing fish may be required to work overtime for 50 days in the year, so it follows that they could be kept on the $64\frac{1}{2}$-hour week for four months consecutively, if required.

In the textile industries the maximum hours of work are more limited, partly because the work is of a more strenuous character than that met with in most other industries. The total hours are limited to $55\frac{1}{2}$ per week and to 10 a day, while no overtime is allowed. On

[1] Ruegg, A. H., and Mossop, L., *The Law of Factories and Workshops*, London, 1902.

Saturdays work lasts from 6 a.m. to 12.30 p.m., if not less than 1 hour is allowed for meals; otherwise, from 6 a.m. to 12 noon, or from 7 a.m. to 1 p.m.

In certain of the seasonal industries the employment of women on overtime for many consecutive weeks is by no means uncommon. In the fruit-canning and jam-preserving industries, since various kinds of fruit ripen successively during the four summer months there may be a continuous rush of work, whilst in the winter months little if any work may be available. In other seasonal work, such as letterpress printing, bookbinding, firewood-cutting, Christmas-present-making, almanac-making, and aerated water manufacture, the rush is usually not so marked, for much of it can be spread over longer periods.

Quite apart from the adverse effects that overtime work may have on health, it ought to be avoided as much as possible on economic grounds. In the first place, it often keeps out of employment some of the numerous band of unemployed persons who are craving for work. Secondly, it is always paid at a higher wage-rate than work in ordinary hours, the rate usually being reckoned as time-and-a-quarter, but sometimes time-and-a-half. Thirdly, it is by no means so productive as the work of ordinary hours, owing to the extra fatigue induced. The classic proof of the ineffectiveness of overtime hours was afforded by Abbé[1] as the result of his observations at the Zeiss optical works, Jena. The output of twelve groups of piece-workers, numbering 233 men in all, was estimated carefully over a period of years, and when the men were working on a nine-hour day they were occasionally required to work one hour a day overtime in seasons of pressure; but it was found that the extra output obtained deteriorated in a week, and by the third or fourth week it was practically non-existent.

[1] Abbé, *Gesammelte Abhandlungen*, Vol. III, p. 226, 1906.

In some observations made by the writer[1] on the output of men engaged in the very strenuous labour of manufacturing tinplates by rolling out red-hot tinplate bars, it was found that when the men were changed from 8-hour shifts to 6-hour shifts their hourly rate of production gradually improved over a period of two months, and then kept fairly steady at an average rate of 11 per cent. above that observed when they were working the longer shifts. When the men were changed back to 8-hour shifts, however, their rate of production fell almost immediately to a value only slightly above that originally observed during the 8-hour shifts, owing to the extra fatigue induced by the longer hours of work. In the less strenuous work performed by most women engaged in industry the fatigue effect induced by the longer hours would probably not develop so suddenly as this, but there can be no doubt that it would soon neutralise a part of the extra production, if not the whole of it.

INTERMITTENT EMPLOYMENT NOT RELATED TO SEASON

In some industries the individual firms are apt to receive large rush orders at any time, and as they have to be completed by a certain date, the available machinery may be insufficient for the purpose unless it is run for an increased number of hours per week by means of the two-shift system. Several firms engaged in manufacturing electric cables have employed considerable numbers of two-shift women on such occupations as covering, braiding and twisting the cables, and there are records of firms where respectively 100, 70, 60 and 40 women, girls and boys were employed on the shift system in 1928.

Of other metal and engineering trades, a firm manu-

---

[1] Vernon, H. M., Report Nos. 1 and 6 of Indust. Fatigue Res. Board, 1919 and 1920.

facturing gramophone motors employed 45 women on intermittent shift work ; one manufacturing cranes and constructional steelwork employed 40 boys ; one manufacturing electrical apparatus (moulding bakelite) employed 40 boys, and two brick-making firms each employed 20 women for putting bricks on the machines.

THE ADMINISTRATION OF ORDERS USED INTERMITTENTLY

When firms use their two-shift Orders intermittently, and especially if they revive them after they have been left in abeyance for a long time, their administration by the factory inspectors becomes rather difficult. The number of factories under the inspectors' charge is so large that, as a rule, they visit them only at infrequent intervals, but the factories adopting the two-shift system receive special attention, and by order of a Home Secretary (Sir W. Joynson-Hicks) they are visited at least once every quarter, if it is known that the system is in operation.[1] Recently-issued Orders contain a request that the inspectorate should be notified when an Order is revived, but this notification is not compulsory, and it has occasionally been found that—unknown to the inspectorate—the two-shift system has been installed or reinstalled by a firm with various unauthorised modifications and extensions. For instance, an Order was obtained owing to seasonal pressure of work, but it was not put into operation till after the lapse of three years. Then, without notification to the Factory Department, it was extended without sanction to a branch works. In another case, where the two-shift system was revived after long disuse the Order itself had been lost, and as the personnel of the management had been changed, no one knew the exact conditions as to meal-times, welfare

[1] *Hansard*, Vol. 222, H.C., Nov. 16th, 1928.

provisions, and the processes covered by the Order. In a third case the two-shift system, which was used intermittently, was applied to a number of young persons less than 16 years of age.

Probably the best method of preventing irregularities in the administration of Orders would be to issue them in two forms. (*a*) Permanent Orders issued as at present, and requiring a fixed standard of welfare provision, such as messroom, cloakroom and washing facilities. If the use of such Orders were intermitted, it should be a legal necessity that their revival should be notified to the Factory Department. (*b*) Temporary Orders quickly obtainable in an emergency for a limited and specified period, in which welfare requirements were less exacting.

In objection to the issue of Temporary Orders it has been urged that it is often impossible to forecast the length of time required for the completion of emergency work; but under such circumstances a fresh Order could be asked for, and this might reasonably contain more stringent welfare conditions than the original Temporary Order.

THE OCCUPATIONS FOR WHICH ORDERS HAVE BEEN OBTAINED

A considerable number of occupations in which the two-shift system has been adopted have been mentioned in this and the two preceding chapters, but they form only a small fraction of the total. A further list is included in the table on page 139, but it makes no pretence to completeness. We see that the occupations indicated are spread widely over various textile and clothing industries; in those of metal manufacture and engineering; in the production of food and of numbers of household goods, and in other miscellaneous occupations. It seems probable, therefore, that the system has been tried at one time or another in almost

OCCUPATIONS FOR WHICH ORDERS HAVE BEEN OBTAINED

Industries.	Occupations, and articles manufactured.
Textiles and clothing	Mule-spinning; weaving on automatic and semi-automatic looms; worsted drawing, spinning, twisting, winding and warping; woollen spinning, weaving and dyeing; cotton doubling, winding and weaving; carding and packing cottonwool; cloth-finishing (print, bleach, dye); chenille-weaving; embroidery (working chain-stitch machines); tape winding and weaving; elastic web-weaving; gauze-weaving; braiding; lace; plain net; bootlaces; glove-making; waterproof clothing; fustian-cutting; carpets; buckram.
Metals and engineering	Railway and tramway rolling-stock; drop stampings and forgings; motor-car parts; electric motors; brake linings; metal window casements; motor-cycle chains; wire fencing; electric bulbs; electric spot welding; safety-razor blades; magnets; electrodes; commutators; dry batteries; tin precipitation; spelter furnace residues; copper department (wire-drawing); umbrella frames; forging pit props.
Food production	Flour-milling; rice-milling; cake and confectionery; sweets and chocolates; sugar-boiling; moulding and packing cheese; whisky-distilling; oil cake; packing flour; jelly-boiling.
Household goods	Enamel plates; enamelled hollow-ware; household brushes; starch; blacklead; pencils; envelopes; candles; soap; toys; telephones; rubber goods; vulcanite and xylonite articles; springs; bedspreads; linoleum.
Miscellaneous	Portland cement; concrete blocks; coke and by-products; briquettes; felt; glue; wood-wool; floor-blocks; tyres; cellulose sheeting; paper-sorting; wood-flour bagging; letterpress printing; racket presses; glass bottles; shoes; millboard; vitreous enamelling; inlay; laundry-work; transporting clay and sand; winding rubber; packing glass bulbs; lithographic printing; preparing hemp; lens grinding and polishing; manufacture and decoration of pottery; asbestos manufacture; making and filling cigarette packets.

every occupation and industry in which women and young persons are employed. This is what would be expected, for there is no reason why a system which is found to be suitable in some occupations should not be almost equally suitable for others. This table of occupations, coupled with those preceding it, suggests that in course of time the system may be extended as a matter of course to almost every industry and occupation in which women and young persons are employed.

When the number of two-shift Orders issued suddenly increased in September, 1931, in consequence of the abandonment of the gold standard, the relative proportion of Orders in textile industries increased to some extent, while that of engineering and miscellaneous industries remained almost the same. The actual number of Orders for industries relating to food production was almost unchanged, so the relative proportion fell considerably, as is indicated by the following data :[1]

PERCENTAGE OF TOTAL ORDERS ISSUED

	Jan. to Aug., 1931.	Sept., 1931, to June, 1932.
Textile and clothing industries	50	56
Metals and engineering	16	14
Food production	10	5
Miscellaneous ...	24	25

THE TWO-SHIFT SYSTEM IN OTHER COUNTRIES

As far as I can ascertain, no legal objections are raised to the adoption of a two-shift system for women in foreign countries, so long as the convention of disallowing work between the hours of 10 p.m. and 5 a.m. is complied with.

[1] *Cf. London Gazette*, 1931–32.

TWO-SHIFT IN INTERMITTENT OPERATION

The shift system has certainly been adopted in many instances, and it is stated[1] that in Germany two- and three-shift systems gained ground in 1921 and 1922, especially when trade was good, but it was found that the period from 6 a.m. to 10 p.m., during which women and young persons may be employed, was not always sufficient. Other instances in which the system has been adopted are in Belgium,[2] where two weaving mills replaced the 10-hour day by an 8-hour day with two shifts. Further instances have been referred to in debates in Parliament. Mr. Rennie Smith said,[3] " I was recently at a large factory at Lodz, the Manchester of Poland, and I found the largest factory there wanting to run, if they could, on the three-shift system and employing girls . . . during the night. Three weeks ago, I was examining a factory at Budapest where they have the two-shift system, but do not only run from 6 to 2, but during the night as well." Mr. Rennie Smith did not definitely state that the night shift at the Budapest factory was worked by women, so it was presumably run by men who worked in conjunction with two day shifts of women, as is done in some English factories. In another Parliamentary debate, Miss Pickford[4] pointed out that, " It is idle to pretend that overhead charges can be brought down so long as our factories and workshops and machinery are standing idle for 12 or 14 hours a day, while those of our competitors are running for 24 hours a day. Surely the only way to bring down the cost of production, to bring down these overhead charges without injury to the workers, is by the fullest and most scientific use of our machinery, and that can be done only if the shift system is allowed."

In the Report on *Hours of Work and Unemployment* recently issued by the International Labour Office at

[1] *Internat. Lab. Rev.* 8, p. 863, 1923.
[2] *The Social Aspects of Rationalisation*, I.L.O., p. 106, 1931.
[3] *Hansard*, Vol. 222, H.C., Nov. 16th, 1928.
[4] *L.c.* Vol. 260, H.C., Nov. 23rd, 1931.

Geneva, several references are made to the two-shift system. Thus it is stated (page 44) that " lack of factory space and plant for the newly-engaged workers could probably be met in most cases by the introduction of any one of the numerous varieties of rotation or shift systems." Again, it is pointed out (page 113) that " the shift system could be adopted on a very wide scale in those establishments which have to remain open for long hours to serve customers. . . . It might also be desirable to consider whether a maximum working week of 42 hours, which would allow for a seven-hour day, would not be preferable, so as to permit the extension of the system of two shifts in the day." The only specific instance given of the adoption of the system relates to a large woollen goods factory in America, where it is stated (page 89) that the staff work in two shifts, the first from 6 a.m. to 2 p.m., and the second from 2 to 10 p.m. No work is done on Saturday, and it is estimated that the plan has allowed the staff to be increased 10 per cent. However, it is stated (page 60) that " in undertakings working with one shift no cases are known of the organisation of a second shift, both shifts working reduced hours." Evidently the writers of the Report were ignorant of the development of the two-shift system in Great Britain, for we have seen that it is almost the invariable custom for the two shifts to work shorter hours than the single shift they replaced. It is true that the system was not adopted, as a rule, with the sole or even the main object of reducing unemployment, but this consideration was clearly present in the mind of many of the employers, and encouraged them to give the system a trial.

THE EMPLOYMENT OF BOYS ON THE TWO-SHIFT SYSTEM

If a firm desires to employ youths aged 16 to 18 on the two-shift system, it is necessary to obtain an Order, but from the age of 18 onwards the youths can, like men, be employed without Orders under any system of day and night shifts that may be required of them. It was stated in a previous chapter that up to December, 1924, over 3,000 boys had been employed at various times on the shift system, or 13 per cent. of the total shift-workers. These boys are useful in certain continuous industries such as glass-bottle manufacture and tinplate manufacture, when linked with a shift of men who work at night from 10 p.m. to 6 a.m. The occupations may be unsuitable for women or girls, so the only alternative would be to employ men on the afternoon shift as well as the night shift.

It was stated earlier in this chapter that one firm employed 40 boys on constructional steelwork, while another employed 40 boys in the manufacture of electrical apparatus. Several other firms, *e.g.*, firms manufacturing Portland cement, cranes, and paper, employed boys on shift work to the exclusion of women, but it appeared to be more usual to employ a small number of boys and a larger number of women and girls. For instance, a yeast-packing firm employed 17 women and 3 boys, a biscuit factory 16 women and 4 boys, and a sugar-packing factory 75 women and 2 boys.

Youths do not appear to be so suitable for shift-work as girls. They are more apt to take advantage of deficient supervision, and at one factory with two shifts of boys the output and quality of the work done was so unsatisfactory that the system soon had to be abandoned.[1] Again, at an engineering factory the lads so frequently asked for permission to leave at 8 p.m. that the afternoon shift was not workable, and had to be abandoned.

Another difficulty relates to the technical evening classes which many of the boys wish to attend. At an electrical engineering works, 50 boys out of the 120 employed were attending such classes, and the firm allowed

[1] *Report of Chief Inspector of Factories for* 1924, p. 53.

the shift-workers time off for these classes, or if this was not possible, it did not put them on to shifts at all. In several other instances the firms were willing to make special arrangements for their boy apprentices, but this plan obviously militated against their suitability for shift-work. The difficulty did not often apply to the girls on shift-work, as it was seldom that any of them wished to attend evening classes. In a few instances, when they did wish to attend, they were transferred to day work. Some of the girls belonged to clubs, but it was no great hardship if the shift-work prevented them from attending on five nights a fortnight.

LIGHTING, HEATING AND VENTILATION UNDER THE TWO-SHIFT SYSTEM

Lighting.—As shift-work extends from 6 a.m. to 10 p.m., while ordinary day work usually runs from 8 a.m. to 5.30 p.m., it follows that the former system necessitates a good many more hours of factory life being spent under conditions of artificial illumination. The artificial lighting of most modern factories is of such a high standard that it throws little, if any, more strain on the eyesight than daylight illumination, but by no means all of our factories have yet introduced the high standard which is so desirable. In spite of this disadvantage, it is probable that shift-workers, taken as a whole, have not much more strain thrown on their eyesight than ordinary day-workers. During some of the winter months the day-workers may have to work in artificial light from 8 to 9 a.m., and again from 3.0 or 3.30 to 5.30 p.m.[1] Except for the dinner hour, they are shut up in the factory for the whole of the daylight hours, and they therefore have to do their home

---

[1] *Cf.* Elton, P. M., Report No. 9 of Indust. Fatigue Res. Board, 1920; Wyatt, S., *l.c.*, Report No. 23, 1923.

work—which includes fine work such as needlework and mending—by artificial light. The shift-workers, on the other hand, have the larger part of the available daylight hours at their disposal when on afternoon shift, and even when they are on morning shift they have two hours or more of daylight between 2 p.m. and dusk. In the summer the shift-workers, when on morning shift, have no work at all by artificial light, and when on afternoon shift they may have less than an hour of it.

Heating.—The complaint is occasionally made that the factories are not sufficiently heated at 6 a.m., when the shift-workers first come on. If this is so, the defect can easily be remedied by starting the stoking of the boiler fires at an earlier hour. They are usually banked up over night, and can be started again at whatever hour the stoker in charge is ordered to attend.

Ventilation.—It is sometimes said that the factory gets very stuffy towards the end of 16 hours' continuous work. If this is so, the ventilation system needs overhauling, for in a well-ventilated factory there is no reason why the air supply and air movement should not be adequate even if the shifts are run continuously.

It is manifest that defects of lighting, heating and ventilation, if they exist, cannot fairly be claimed as an argument against the two-shift system. They are extraneous conditions which can be remedied and ought to be remedied wherever they are found to exist, whatever the shift system in force.

CHAPTER VII

THE OPINIONS OF THE WORKERS AND OTHERS ON THE TWO-SHIFT SYSTEM

CONTENTS

The Opinions of the Workers—Labour Turnover—The Opinions of Managers, Supervisors and Parents—The Opinions of Workers' Organisations—Opinions Expressed in Parliament—General Conclusions

THE OPINIONS OF THE WORKERS

WHATEVER the merits of the two-shift system on economic grounds, it is not likely to be widely adopted if it is seriously opposed by the women who have to work under it. It is, therefore, most important to ascertain their opinions, and repeated efforts have been made by the factory inspectors and other investigators to discover what they really think about the system. It is sometimes found that the workers, when questioned, are afraid to give their genuine views, for fear that they may get into bad favour with the management, so the inspectors have tried to gain their confidence by getting into informal conversation with them when suitable opportunities offered. By talking to them individually about their work in its various aspects the inspectors were able to obtain a shrewd idea of their real thoughts.

The Annual Reports of the Chief Inspector of Factories discuss the views of the workers on a number of occasions. As might be expected, there are wide divergences of opinion, and one inspector reports[1] that in the Southern

[1] Report of Chief Inspector of Factories for 1922, p. 53.

Division " the attitude of the workers varies . . . from enthusiastic approval to reluctant acquiescence." Another inspector reports that in the Scotland Division there was " perfect contentment with the two-shift system on the part of those women who have been working under it for an unbroken period of seven years, which began in wartime," but in two other divisions it is reported that the majority of the workers prefer the ordinary day shift.

In the North-Eastern and North Midland Divisions, where shift-work for men has prevailed for generations in lace manufacture, the iron and steel trades, mining and other staple industries, and where, in consequence, home life is already organised so as to accord with the shift system, most of the women appear to be well satisfied with the shifts, once they have become accustomed to them.[1] It is generally reported that in factories where both day-work and shift-work are carried on the day-workers often apply to be put on shift-work, but not *vice versa*. On the other hand, in some factories where the system has been running for a fairly long time, part of the women liked the system at first, but have since tired of it. In a subsequent report[2] concerning these two divisions the inspector says that, " In no case have I found real antipathy to the system on the part of the workers," while another inspector (South London) mentions a case where it is considered to be promotion to get on to shift-work.

In the Eastern Division it is reported[3] that " although some women prefer to work on shifts the majority prefer ordinary day-work."

The previously-mentioned investigators of the Industrial Fatigue Research Board collected information systematically at four factories, and they obtained striking

[1] Report of Chief Inspector of Factories for 1924, p. 54.
[2] Report for 1927, p. 59.
[3] Report for 1931, p. 58.

evidence of the importance of habit in determining opinion. They state[1] that at Factory C (paper bags), where the system has been in operation for some years, 90 per cent. of the workers preferred shift-work. At Factory A (artificial silk), where the majority of the workers questioned had been on shift-work for some time, three-quarters of them preferred shift-work. At Factory B (electrical engineering), where the majority of the workers had been on shift-work for six months or less, 90 per cent. of those questioned preferred day-work. At Factory D (wire-drawing) the workers who had been on shift-work for some years said that they preferred shift-work. Those who were formerly on shift-work, but had been transferred to day-work for about a year, said that they preferred day-work. Frequently they could give no reason for their preference, while some of them merely said that they were used to it.

At a factory where electric cables were manufactured a group of 16 women were questioned after they had been working on the shift system for 3 to 14 weeks, and they were unanimous in saying that they disliked it; but when the same women were questioned again a few months later, six of them said that they preferred the shift system, while two were indifferent.

The results of questioning small numbers of workers engaged on various occupations, at factories situated in localities distributed all over the country, are classified in the table on page 149. Unfortunately no information is available as to the times for which these workers had been employed on shift-work, but taking the data for what they are worth, we see that in about a third of all the factories a considerable majority of the workers preferred shift-work, while in another third they preferred day-work. Of the total of 438 workers questioned, 215, or just under half,

---

[1] Smith, M. and Vernon, M. D., Report No. 47 of Indust. Fatigue Res. Board, p. 30.

preferred shift-work, while 58 were indifferent. Some of these indifferent workers said that they had got used to the system, and had no preference either way.

The reasons for the preferences given by the women

OPINIONS OF THE WORKERS ON THE SHIFT SYSTEM

Factories where the workers questioned were :	In favour of shifts.	Indifferent.	In favour of day-work.
(a) Mostly in favour of shifts	70, 36, 17, 22, 8, 10 } 163	4, 5, 6, 4, 5, 0 } 24	15, 1, 10, 15, 1, 1 } 43
(b) Fairly evenly balanced	11, 6, 6, 4 } 27	7, 12, 2, 0 } 21	12, 8, 8, 5 } 33
(c) Mostly in favour of day-work	3, 9, 6, 3, 4 } 25	0, 1, 6, 1, 5 } 13	45, 13, 12, 11, 8 } 89
	215	58	165

working in various factories were very similar, and most of them could be classified under one of half a dozen headings. Some of the women questioned gave more than one reason, so they have been entered twice in the next table, while others gave no reasons at all and are therefore omitted. Hence these data do not show a numerical correspondence with those of the preceding table. The answers for and against shift-work almost balance, and we see that the chief reason for the shift-work preference was that the system afforded more free time as the hours of work were shorter. The chief reason for day-work preference was that it left all the evenings free. Early rising was not objected to nearly so much as the loss of the evenings, though it should be remembered that Saturday evening was always free. Of the workers who preferred the shift system, 74 per cent. were found to like working

Preferences for shift-work	More free time ... ... 128 Less tiring owing to shorter hours 43 Variety due to change of shifts... 26	197
Preferences for day-work	All the evenings free ... ... 95 Later rising and more sleep ... 55 Regular hours and meal-times; better for health 45	195

on the morning shift better than on the afternoon shift. The reason given in almost all cases was that it left the evenings free, though a few of the women said that they found the morning shifts to be less tiring. Sometimes the reasons given for the dislike of the afternoon shifts were rather pathetic. Several girls found that their sweethearts were apt to go courting elsewhere on the evenings when they were at work, and one of them said frankly, "I am courting." Another said that her sweetheart did not like coming to meet her so late as 10 p.m. For these and other social reasons, such as visits to dance halls, cinemas, and girls' clubs, it is the young women who chiefly object to the afternoon shifts. The married women more often than not prefer them, as they can attend to their household duties in the mornings.

In some instances the preferences were stronger than those suggested by the table. At one artificial silk factory the girls were eager to go on to shift-work, while at another they volunteered to go on it. At a third silk factory, where the shift system was tried and given up, there was a clamorous demand that it should be continued. At one factory it was found that women came from other factories, where they were on day-work, hoping to get put on shift-work. At another, where the shift system was worked intermittently, the operatives termed the period of shift-work the " rest weeks," as they felt so much fresher than when they were on day-work.

On the other hand, the dislikes to the shift system were occasionally expressed even more emphatically than the likes. One woman said that shift-work was " rotten," as she had to be up at 4.45 a.m., and got no proper meals. Another was " fed up with shift-work." Another said that the afternoon shift was " no good; it drags "; another—who did a good deal of home work—that the shift system seems " all work."

THE LABOUR TURNOVER

We have seen that the two-shift system possesses certain advantages and certain disadvantages. If the disadvantages are held to outweigh the advantages substantially, the women employed generally seek work at some other factory where the shift system is not in operation. The labour turnover at a factory, therefore, affords some index of the favour in which the system is held, and in many cases it is a surprisingly sensitive index. For instance, at two large confectionery and cocoa factories situated in the same district in London, it was found that while 52 per cent. of the workers left every year from one factory, no less than 94 per cent. left from the other one.[1] The reasons of the huge turnover in the latter factory appeared to be that there was not, as in the former factory, a brief rest pause of three minutes' duration in the middle of each

[1] Vernon, H. M., Vernon, M. D., and Lorrain-Smith, I., Report No. 47 of Indust. Fatigue Res. Board, 1928, p. 4.

work spell, during which a cup of tea was offered to every worker. In a third confectionery factory situated in another district in London the labour turnover was only 21 per cent. per annum, possibly because the women were allowed a 15-minute rest pause in each work spell, during which they went to the canteen.

The investigators of the Industrial Fatigue Research Board were able to study in some detail the labour turnover at the large artificial silk factory previously mentioned. They found[1] that, on an average, out of the 1,600 workers investigated about half left every year. When the women were classified according to the departments in which they were working, the following annual turnover was observed for each 100 employees:

Departments always on shift-work	47
,, ,, ,, day-work	30
,, changing from shift- to day-work, or *vice versa*, during the year	77

It will be seen that the labour turnover was half as great again in the departments always on shift-work as in those always on day-work; but when the results were calculated on a monthly basis it was found that the difference of turnover was not significant in the strict statistical sense, as it was only $1·5 \pm 0·66$ per month per 100 workers. In the departments where there was a change over from one system to the other the turnover was, however, more than two and a half times greater than in the departments always on day-work. (This difference amounted to $4·0 \pm 0·66$ per month, and is therefore statistically significant.) There can be no doubt, therefore, that the unsettled conditions were strongly disapproved of, and were largely responsible for the big turnover. It was found that three-fourths of the

[1] Smith, M., and Vernon, M. D., *l.c.*, p. 28.

women who left did so at their own request, and not because the firm discharged them.

The large labour turnover observed at the several factories mentioned is an index of what happens in many if not most other factories. It is an unsatisfactory state of affairs, for it implies that there is a considerable floating labour market, involving much unemployment with consequent unrest and anxiety. The turnover of the men is usually smaller than that of the women, but even among them it is regrettably large.

THE OPINIONS OF MANAGERS, SUPERVISORS AND PARENTS

The Opinions of the Managerial Staff.—The opinions of the employers on the merits of the two-shift system have been discussed in a previous chapter, but it is desirable that the views of the managerial staff should also be referred to. These views naturally vary considerably in the factories where the two-shift system is organised on a large and fairly complete scale, and in those where there are comparatively few shift-workers, or where they are employed intermittently. If there is a large and permanent double shift it is worth while for the employers to duplicate most of their supervisory staff of managers, foremen, charge hands, mechanics, repair men and others in charge. This is what was done during the war in many of the munition factories, where night shifts were worked regularly. Such a complete duplication of staff may be difficult to achieve, as it may not be easy to find suitable men, and in any case it is very expensive. In practice it is found that, as a rule, there is no duplication of most of the staff, but some of those in charge have to work considerably longer hours than should reasonably be expected of them. For instance, it was reported that in many cases occupiers, managers and foremen had to be present from 12 to 16 hours a day for supervision, and perhaps longer for repairs. The alternative is to allow the supervision to become defective, or even completely lacking, during most of the morning period between 6 and 8 a.m., and the evening period from 6 to 10 p.m., when the shift-workers are working alone.

Reports received from a number of independent sources agree in indicating that, for the reasons stated, the two-shift system is usually unpopular with the managerial and supervisory staff. Nevertheless this unpopularity can be very largely avoided by careful organisation and the duplication of a portion of the staff. If this duplication is considered to be too expensive, the shift system ought to be given up, except for short rush periods.

The Opinions of Parents.—Scarcely less important than the opinions of the managerial staff on the shift system are those of the parents and guardians of the women and young persons concerned. It is impossible to ascertain these opinions with any approach to fairness and impartiality, as it is almost always the objectors to the system who are most outspoken in airing their views, whereas those who have no objection, or who acquiesce in it, remain silent. Nevertheless, it should be realised that strong objections are held in some cases, even though we may not be able to estimate their importance.

In a Parliamentary debate on the two-shift system, held in 1928, Miss Bondfield said,[1] " I am authorised to speak to-day on behalf of a very large number of women's organisations which have not only held conferences, but have repeatedly passed resolutions from the standpoint of the mothers of those young girls. . . . I have some very pathetic letters . . . which have been written to me as chief woman officer of my own trade union." Miss Bondfield then read the following letters :

(*a*) " In view of the proposed alteration of shift-work at

[1] *Hansard*, Vol. 222, H.C., Nov. 16th, 1928.

OPINIONS OF THE WORKERS

Hardy and Hinde's silk factory, namely 6 a.m. to 2 p.m. and 2 p.m. to 10 p.m., as a parent I strongly object to this proposition. Both morally and physically the hours are not good for young people. I sincerely hope that you will do all in your power to resist this introduction."

(b) "I am writing concerning the shift system, which all sensible mothers strongly object to. I sincerely trust that Mr. Hardy will think twice before he forces this unwelcome system upon his workers, who are willing to work anywhere at proper hours."

(c) "I am writing a few lines in regard to Mr. Hardy's silk works, as I hear that the girls have to go on shifts which I object to. I have been a weaver myself 46 years ago, and quite understand what it is to get up at five o'clock in the mornings, roughing all weathers; also being deprived of all their social evenings through working till late at night, which makes them good for nothing. When they reach home after eleven it also means that it is ruining their health, and I do not think that it is fair to the girls."

It will be noted that all three letters relate to the same factory, so it is probable that their origin was inspired by a common source. They do not adduce any evidence of harm actually done to the girls, but only of what the mothers expect to happen. The writer of letter (c) refers to what she herself experienced as a weaver, but she would have been on a 10-hour day with a 6 a.m. start throughout the year, a very different set of conditions from a $7\frac{1}{2}$-hour day and a 6 a.m. start in alternate weeks. Miss Bondfield said further, "I have a number of other letters from mothers in which they make reference to the injury done to health of their daughters." It is a pity that she did not read some of them instead of those above quoted, but in any case they could scarcely be held to outweigh the statistical evidence of health effects recorded in a previous chapter.

THE OPINIONS OF WORKERS' ORGANISATIONS

The workers' organisations are greatly divided in their opinions about the two-shift system. It is generally found that while the local branches of the trade unions encourage the application for Orders, the headquarters oppose them.[1] In one case it was alleged that coercion had been brought to bear on the workers, but this was proved to be without foundation.[2] In another case, when a similar complaint was made, the inspector arranged a meeting between the occupier of the factory and the representative of the workers' organisation, and a new agreement as to wages was arrived at which resulted in a withdrawal of the representatives' objection.[3]

The opposition of some of the trade unions in the textile industries is specially strong. It appears to be due in part to the fear that the introduction of a 6 a.m. start for the shift-workers may ultimately cause, for all the workers, a reversion to the early start which was in vogue before the war, and to the $55\frac{1}{2}$-hour week. It is also thought that it may lead to the introduction of night shifts for men in occupations and industries which have hitherto been free from it. Again, there is a feeling that the men's wages may be lowered if the facilities for women's employment are increased. In a Parliamentary debate on the two-shift system held in 1931,[4] a Labour member (Mr. J. Jones) said frankly, "If industry can be so organised that we can bring men back into employment, every man brought back into industry is a greater gain to the State than merely keeping women employed in the factories and workshops under present conditions." Major Salmon, in reply, said that Mr. Jones "first told us that it does not matter if you throw out the women so long as you employ the men, and

---

[1] Report of Chief Inspector of Factories for 1924, p. 54.
[2] Report for 1931, p. 59.
[3] *L.c.*
[4] *Hansard*, Vol. 260, H.C., Nov. 23rd, 1931.

then that the two-shift system necessarily means the employment of fewer people."

It is said that the two-shift system is not readily adaptable to textile processes, owing to the lack of uniformity in a product which is the joint work of different operatives, and to the difficulty of estimating their wages on a piece-work basis. However, these difficulties appear to have been overcome in the artificial silk industry. In one instance the decision to adopt the system in an artificial silk-spinning mill was taken in full consultation with the trade union, for it was found that it led to an increase of employment, not only in the mill concerned, but in a weaving mill in another village, which had been on short time owing to difficulty in getting adequate supplies of spun silk.

In one industry the adoption of the system had to be given up as the trade union insisted that the workers should be paid for part of their second shift at overtime rates. In a number of instances the opposition of the trade unions has been so strong that the employers have not thought it worth their while to antagonise them by proceeding with their plans for introducing the system.

The opposition of the trade unions, as voiced in Parliament, appears to depend largely on their contention that they ought to be consulted officially by the Home Office before any two-shift Order is granted. Mr. Rhys Davies said,[1] " The Home Secretary has been asked to make it possible for the consent of the workpeople to be obtained through their trade union, and he has stated again and again in response that he has no power to enforce such a provision. I feel sure that the Committee will agree . . . that the ballot vote ought to be conducted in conjunction with the trade union concerned instead of being allowed to be dealt with by the employer and the workpeople alone." Mr. Davies said further that the trade unions

[1] *Hansard*, Vol. 260, H.C., Nov. 23rd, 1931.

object to the two-shift system on the following grounds:
" That it upsets family and social life, and that it increases the cost of providing cooked meals for members of the same family coming in at different hours of the day and night. . . . That the hours of labour under the system are out of harmony with the working day of other operatives living in the area and doing similar work; that the system has developed just in proportion to the necessity for its curtailment. . . . There has been an extension of the system just in proportion to the increase of unemployment in the country. One factory in a town may adopt the two-shift system and work at top speed, making it impossible for another factory in the same town to find work at all."

Major Salmon, speaking in reply, pointed out that Mr. Davies' demand as a condition of the continuance of the two-shift system was " Let the trade unions manage it, and that those who are not in the trade unions must come in if they want to go on with the two-shift system. In other words, he wants to treat this as a means of getting back to the trade union movement the numbers that, as he has suggested, they have lost recently." Again, Mr. Stanley pointed out that the claim that the consent of the trade unions should first be obtained is, " from the point of view of the practicability of such a course, to ignore entirely the circumstances in which such Orders are usually required. In most cases they are wanted as a matter of great urgency." He said that to insist on a previous application to a trade union " would impose an intolerable delay and in many cases largely nullify the advantage which this two-shift Order gives."

If an industry possesses a joint industrial council, it has the legal right to prevent the issue of an Order by the Home Secretary. Thus the Home Secretary (Sir W. Joynson-Hicks) stated in Parliament,[1] " If the Industrial

[1] *Hansard*, Vol. 211, H.C., Dec. 13th, 1927.

Council, on joint representations being made by organisations representing a majority of employers and workers in the industry concerned, or the section of the industry concerned, represents to the Secretary of State that the Orders ought not to be made, the powers of the Secretary of State cease." It appears that some of the industrial councils wish to extend their powers beyond their legal rights, for Mr. Mackinder, a Labour member, said[1] that a council in which he was interested " feel that it is they and they alone who ought to have the right to give permission to work the two-shift system. They are on the spot . . . they know the firms and the conditions of employment, they know the good employers and the bad employers . . . and with the information at their disposal, they ought to have the right and the power to issue permits for allowing girls to work on the two-shift system, on the application of an employer."

In a previous debate[2] Mr. Mackinder said that " The Woven Allied Textile Council, at a meeting of employers and workpeople, passed a resolution instructing their secretary to ask this factory to cease working the two-shift system." The Home Secretary pointed out in reply that " there has been no complaint even from the local trade unions. . . . I challenge the hon. member to send me any evidence that the local trade union branch, of which these workpeople are members, have sent any complaint to the Home Office, regarding the working of any Order which I have made."

Another objection advanced by the trade unions is that their union meetings would be interfered with.[3] Such meetings are usually held in the evenings, after the day's work is over, and if the second shift continued till 9 or 10 p.m. it would not be possible for the workers in this

---

[1] *L.c.* Vol. 222, H.C., Nov. 16th, 1928.
[2] *L.c.* Vol. 211, H.C., Dec. 13th, 1927.
[3] *The Organiser*, Feb., 1918.

shift to attend. The difficulty does not appear to be a serious one, for in any case the Saturday evening is free for everyone, and if a meeting were desired on some other evening it is probable that the afternoon shift would be able to get permission to stop work an hour or two earlier than usual in order to attend it.

There may be other and better reasons than those cited for the opposition of the trade unions to the two-shift system, but I have been unable to ascertain them. In a debate on the system held at Bradford in 1929, it was reported[1] that " the trade unions are strongly opposed to this system in the textile trade, but steadily refuse to say why. . . . Nothing would induce those unionists present to give a reason for their opposition." It is obvious that a good deal of this opposition is due to unreasoning prejudice, but it cannot be denied that a wide extension of the shift system might possibly lead to some increase of night work for men. It is universally admitted that industry is becoming more and more mechanised, and that the overhead costs of elaborate machinery tend to become greater and greater. If, on the two-shift system, it is found to be an economic advantage to run this machinery for 16 hours a day instead of the usual 8 or 9 hours, as at present, it would be a still greater advantage to run it continuously for the whole 24 hours. Nevertheless, the increasing mechanism in the continuous industries which already employ a regular night shift may possibly set free more men from night work than would be needed to control the freshly-arranged night work in other industries.

The reversion of workers in general to a $55\frac{1}{2}$-hour week and a 6 a.m. start is so improbable that it is not worth discussing, but the tendency to the increased substitution of women for men in industry can scarcely be denied. If, however, industry as a whole is in a prosperous and healthy condition it ought to be possible to absorb nearly all the

[1] *Welfare Work*, Jan., 1929, p. 12.

OPINIONS OF THE WORKERS

available labour, especially if the men, as well as the women, work on shifts of $7\frac{1}{2}$, 7 or even 6 hours' duration.

OPINIONS EXPRESSED IN PARLIAMENT

During the last few years the question of the renewal of the section of the Act permitting the Home Secretary to grant two-shift Orders has had to be brought forward annually in Parliament under the Expiring Laws Continuance Bill, and a lively debate is generally initiated by some of the Labour members. Several of these debates have been referred to in the previous section. Mr. Rhys Davies is a particularly active opponent of the system, and on several occasions he has moved an amendment to the effect that the clause of the Bill relating to the renewal of the section of the Act in question should be deleted. He said,[1] " Are we not proceeding to the stage when practically all employers of labour engaged in factory work will claim that the two-shift system shall become universal ? . . . These Orders can be cancelled without inflicting any hardship whatever on the owners. . . . The two-shift system should be abandoned because it upsets the domestic arrangements of the workers and their families." Mr. T. Shaw spoke still more emphatically against the proposed renewal, for he said, " In Lancashire for a century our people have worked to change a state of things that stank in the nostrils, to guarantee women and children against certain conditions. The Home Secretary, by his methods, is raising the danger in Lancashire that if a body of workpeople can be found foolish enough to demand the two-shift system, he can bring our work of a century to an end. . . . At ten years of age I began it (viz., work at 6 a.m.), and my experience of it has led me to say that no child of mine, if I could avoid it, should do it, because I

---

[1] *Hansard*, Vol. 222, H.C., Nov. 16th, 1928.

believe it to be inhuman, and what I do not want for my own wife or for my own daughter I do not want for any other man's wife or daughter." In a subsequent debate Mr. Shaw said, " In my opinion, no civilised nation will allow its girls and women to get up at half-past five on a winter's morning to go to work."

It will be generally admitted that it is unpleasant to get up and go to work on cold and dark mornings in the winter at 5.30 a.m., but it should be remembered that during two or three of the winter months it is almost as cold and dark at 7.0 to 7.30 a.m. as at 5.30 a.m.; yet nearly all other industrial workers have to proceed to work at this time. The shift-workers have at least the solace—denied to other workers—of lying in bed till 9 a.m. or later in alternate weeks, and we saw in the previous chapter that the majority of them prefer the morning shift to the afternoon shift.

In the years when the Labour Government was in power, the overt opposition of the Labour members to the Act dwindled almost to zero. It is true that Mr. Clynes, the Home Secretary, said[1] that he agreed with Mr. Kelly (a member who proposed the omission of the clause relating to the Act from the Expiring Laws Continuance Bill) in objecting to the two-shift system, but the course suggested would " tend seriously to dislocate industrial relations and impose real hardships upon a very large number of people." In the debate held in the following year, Mr. Short (the Under-Secretary for Home Affairs) pointed out[2] that " if the two-shift system was brought to an end this year it would mean grave dislocation and would no doubt contribute to the industrial depression."

The next annual debate occurred when the National Government was in power, and Mr. Rhys Davies,[3] when

---

[1] *Hansard*, Vol. 232, H.C., Nov. 26th, 1929.
[2] *L.c.* Vol. 245, Dec. 4th, 1930.
[3] *L.c.* Vol. 260, Nov. 23rd, 1931.

moving an amendment to omit the clause relating to the two-shift system, explained that the Labour Government had not taken steps to remove the clause when they were in office as it had not sufficient backing to carry anything through the House. His contention was, however, contradicted by another Labour member (Mr. Tinker), who admitted that his Government "had the opportunity of making this alteration in the law and that we did not do so. I agree that this is a strong point." The point in question was referred to by Mr. Stanley[1] (the Under-Secretary of State for Home Affairs) in the 1932 debate, when he was explaining the sudden increase of Orders granted in the autumn of 1931. He said, " When he (Mr. Rhys Davies) tells us that this system was never meant to be anything but temporary, and that it was intended by Parliament that it should come to an end three or four years ago, I can only remind him that of the three or four years by which its life exceeded the contemplation of Parliament, two or three were under the auspices of a Government of the party to which the hon. member himself belongs. The number of Orders granted under the two-shift system, within the tenure of office of the Labour Government, was only limited by the lack of applications and not by that Government's dislike of them or refusal to grant them. The reason, of course, for the sudden increase in recent months is not any change of policy on the part of the Home Office with regard to the granting of these applications. It has resulted from the tremendous increase in the number of applications which followed leaving the Gold Standard, and the sudden impetus then given to the export trade, particularly in the textile industry. This meant that orders for goods were given suddenly and had to be executed or else refused. It enables firms to execute rush orders by working in two shifts instead of working overtime. It enables an industry,

[1] *L.c.* Vol. 268, July 6th, 1932.

such as the textile industry, which is suddenly faced with rush orders to fill these orders on existing machinery and not to embark on the installation of further machinery until they are assured that the sudden impetus has something continuing behind it and is going to result in a lasting improvement which will justify such an installation."

GENERAL CONCLUSIONS

A detailed description of the two-shift system has been given in the present chapter and those preceding it because it appears to the writer that it ought to be considered seriously and impartially by all employers of labour. They are, almost without exception, interested in the question of hours of work, for they know that their employees are asking, with more and more persistence, for a reduction in these hours, coupled with the maintenance of full wages, and they know, or should know, that industry, if properly organised, can easily afford to pay good wages even if the hours of work are considerably curtailed.

Though the two-shift system can be applied without any restrictions or legal formalities to any occupation worked solely by men and youths aged 18 years and upwards, such occupations are probably in the minority, so the legally-sanctioned two-shift Orders would usually have to be applied for. The youths begin work at the age of 14 to 16, and it may be found a great convenience to be able to employ some of them on a shift system when necessary, *e.g.*, in such industries as glass-bottle-making and the tinplate trade.

Industrial occupations as a whole are tending to become more and more of a repetition character, and women are much better suited to light repetitive work than men as they are less affected by its monotony. For these and other reasons women are likely to penetrate more and more into industry and to work in conjunction with the men. The men will perform the heavier tasks, and act as skilled mechanics; but since they usually work for the same hours as the women, the two-shift system, if adopted for the women, will apply to the men as well.

As has already been pointed out, one of the great advantages of the two-shift system lies in its elasticity. Once the principle of two 8-hour shifts a day has been adopted as a logical successor to the one-shift 48-hour week, it will be easy to relax the hours of work gradually by half-hour stages. The $7\frac{1}{2}$ hours of actual work can first be cut down to 7 hours for the morning shift only, whereby it will be possible to begin this shift at 6.30 a.m. instead of 6 a.m. Next the afternoon shift can be reduced to 7 hours, whereby the evening shift can be finished at 9.30 p.m.; or alternatively, the morning shift can be started at 7 a.m. and the evening shift be finished at 10 p.m. as at present. Subsequent reductions to $6\frac{1}{2}$ and to 6 hours of work per shift would enable the morning shift to be started at 7, 7.30 or 8 a.m., according to the time at which the evening shift was finished, so the objections of the shift-workers to very early rising would be overcome.

As the shift system becomes more general, it may be found possible to relax some of the legal formalities now involved in its application, and especially so if the hours of work are cut down to $6\frac{1}{2}$ per shift, with the consequent 7 a.m. start and 9 p.m. finish. It is to be hoped that whatever the relaxations allowed the welfare provisions will still be maintained, and that good cloakroom and mess-room accommodation, coupled with adequate washing facilities, will be insisted upon.

So far the two-shift system has, with few exceptions, been adopted only in the manufacturing industries which fall under the control of the Factory Department of the Home Office, but there is no reason why the system should not be applied to other industries and occupations. In shops where the working day sometimes extends from 9 a.m. to 10 p.m. a two-shift system might be adopted for some of the employees, and the very long hours sometimes worked in the hotel and catering trade might well be relieved by the adoption of the system.

With regard to occupations in which men alone are employed, it is to be hoped that the extension of the shift system in manufacturing industries will lead to its being copied for road transport workers and other distributors. Some drivers of motor vehicles are compelled to work for such long hours that the over-fatigue induced has led to fatal accidents.

In agriculture two shifts could be worked in summer, and would be especially useful in rush periods such as harvest time. An eight-hour day is sufficient for the drivers of motor tractors and harvesters, and there would be sufficient daylight to run two shifts during several of the summer months. The difficulty would be to find work for some of the shift-workers in the winter.

CHAPTER VIII

THE PROBLEM OF LEISURE

CONTENTS

Introduction—Evidence of the Use to which Leisure Hours are Put—The Best Use of Leisure—Leisure and the Two-Shift System—Leisure and the Unemployed—How Other Countries Meet the Problem of Leisure—General Conclusions

INTRODUCTION

A REDUCTION in the weekly hours of work implies a corresponding increase in the hours of leisure, and the problem of occupying these hours wisely becomes one of increasing importance. As industrial work tends to become progressively more monotonous in character, the workers look more and more to the activities of their leisure hours for the fulfilment of their desire for a happy life. Rightly occupied, their leisure hours should give them variety and interests which compensate for the dullness inevitably attaching to most routine work.

Dr. Dyson, Master of Music at Winchester College, in a presidential address before the annual conference of Educational Associations,[1] pointed out that it was generally agreed that proficiency in reading, writing and arithmetic must be acquired by all young people, while certain other subjects such as Latin, algebra and chemistry were held to be essential preliminaries to higher education. Yet arts and crafts such as painting, music and skilled mechanical work were looked upon as frills, though in many respects the arts and crafts would appear to be

[1] *The Times*, Jan. 2nd, 1934.

above all others the most suitable training grounds both for the serious business of life and for the leisure and recreation which might diversify that life. Most of our children would have to earn their bread by tasks which would deaden rather than quicken their faculties, and we consequently had to educate not so much for work as for leisure. It was here that the educational pursuit of the arts and crafts should step in. Nothing was more urgent in our time than a change in the whole psychology of work and leisure, and every child ought to be taught arts and handicrafts without stint.

The choice of occupations for leisure hours necessarily depends on the facilities offered. The wider the range of occupations available the greater the probability that the worker will select those which will afford him the highest degree of ultimate satisfaction. When there is very little choice at his disposal he is apt to drift into such channels of amusement and distraction as are immediately at hand, and to neglect those which need some effort for their pursuit. It follows that the adequate fulfilment of the possibilities of leisure hours depends to a considerable extent on the careful organisation of schemes for leisure occupations, and for disinterested assistance by voluntary helpers in running such schemes.

EVIDENCE OF THE USE TO WHICH LEISURE HOURS ARE PUT

The occupations indulged in during leisure hours are innumerable, and no two persons choose alike. Nevertheless, the small amount of information available suggests that there is usually a good deal of similarity in the leisure-hour occupations of persons of the same social class who are living in the same district and are employed on somewhat similar types of industrial work. These occupations

THE PROBLEM OF LEISURE 169

can be roughly ascertained by statistical enquiry, and an investigation of this character is described in the previously-mentioned report on *New Aspects of the Problem of Hours of Work*. A questionnaire was issued to 1,500 working men and women in Liverpool, and replies were received from 90 persons of each sex. Three-fourths of the men were under 40 years of age, while nine-tenths of the women were under 30. They were all working on a

AVERAGE DISTRIBUTION OF TOTAL HOURS PER WEEK

	Men.	Women.
At work	48	48
In transit to or from work	9	9
Meals and personal matters	21	21
Sleep	55	60
Balance of leisure	35	30
Total hours in the week	168	168

48-hour week, and the above table shows the average distribution of the total weekly hours at their disposal.

It will be seen that the men averaged 35 hours of leisure per week, and the women 30 hours. These hours were distributed in the ways shown in the table on page 170.

This table shows that about half of all the leisure hours concerning which information was vouchsafed were spent in amusements and recreations. No mention is made of visits to public-houses, but it has been stated[1] that well over half the adult population of the country frequent these institutions, and as eleven hours of the men's leisure were unaccounted for, it is reasonable to suppose that they

[1] Selley, E., *The English Public-house As It Is*, London, 1927.

were to a large extent utilised in this manner. All the persons interrogated spent some portion of their time on amusements and recreations, and the table indicates that 72 per cent. of the men and women spent over three hours each in attending religious services. The other occupations

USE OF LEISURE HOURS

Occupation.	Men.			Women.		
	Per cent. of persons so engaged.	Average hours spent by persons so engaged.	Average hours spent by whole group.	Per cent. of persons so engaged.	Average hours spent by persons so engaged.	Average hours spent by whole group.
Amusements	77	5·5	4·3	93	4·4	4·1
Recreations	97	11·0	10·7	98	10·1	9·9
Hobbies	29	5·7	1·4	7	1·5	0·1
Educational	40	4·2	1·7	25	2·6	0·6
Helping in the home	33	3·3	1·1	72	5·4	3·9
Social visits	41	3·5	1·5	54	5·0	2·7
Religious services	72	3·3	2·4	72	3·5	2·6
Social work	26	3·1	0·8	18	2·7	0·5
Unaccounted for			11·1			5·6
Total hours of leisure per week			35·0			30·0

were, with one exception, indulged in by only a minority of the workers. Hence the time expended on them, though usually substantial, fell off greatly when averaged over the whole group. Of the amusements and recreations indulged in, the great majority were indoors, as can be seen from the next table, page 171.

Probably the persons represented in these tables are a select group, as they represent the small fraction of the total number of persons questioned who took the trouble

THE PROBLEM OF LEISURE

to reply. It seems likely that they were superior to the average in their desire for educational and useful pursuits. The lack of desire for self-improvement and usefulness is suggested by an estimate made by another investigator,[1] which was based on records of attendances at cinemas,

RECREATIONS AND AMUSEMENTS

Occupation.	Men.		Women.	
	Per cent. of persons so engaged.	Average hours spent by persons so engaged.	Per cent. of persons so engaged.	Average hours spent by persons so engaged.
Indoors:				
Cinema or theatre	64	3·5	76	3·7
Listening to music	36	4·5	44	2·5
Music-playing	9	3·0	30	1·8
Dancing	6	4·6	17	3·9
Reading	83	4·4	84	4·4
Social gatherings	15	4·3	13	2·6
Games	34	2·5	28	2·3
Out of doors:				
Watching games	19	2·4	7	1·7
Playing games	18	4·2	19	2·2
Walking, cycling	78	5·4	74	5·0

public-houses and educational establishments in the country as a whole. It likewise indicated that the hours of leisure of employed persons amounted to from 30 to 35 hours a week. Out of the 35 hours 3 were spent at cinemas and 3 at public-houses, and only 6 minutes a week, on an average, or 0·3 per cent. of the total time, at educational establishments.

Another set of statistics,[2] collected by an American Recreational Association, leads to a similar conclusion

[1] *L.c.* p. 8.
[2] *Internat. Lab. Rev.*, 9, p. 896, 1924.

about education. The data in the table represent the spare-time activities most desired by the employees in shops and stores in Pennsylvania, and it will be seen that

SPARE-TIME ACTIVITIES DESIRED BY EMPLOYEES IN SHOPS IN U.S.A.

Physical recreations, 2,880	Baseball	548	Useful indoor pursuits, 635	Dressmaking	210
	Swimming	484		Costume-designing	153
	Skating	331		Cooking	97
	Bowling	325		Millinery	79
	Basketball	309		Basketry	56
	Tennis	238		Pottery	30
	Gymnasium	238			
	Hiking	237			
	Golf	91			
	Volley ball	79			
Indoor social recreations, 1,174	Dancing	504	Educational and altruistic 328	First aid	166
	Social club	211		Girls' club work	69
	Singing club	160		Boys' club work	34
	Ukulele club	121		Social hygiene	32
	Glee club	89		Dramatic study	27
	Dramatic playing	89	Miscellaneous		40

less than a fifth of all the employees desired to employ their free time on useful indoor pursuits, or on educational and altruistic work. Over half of them wanted outdoor physical recreation in some form, a natural consequence of their being shut up all day in their shops.

Leisure in Relation to Instincts.—It is pointed out by Prof. Burt[1] that the chief motive for amusement in leisure hours is the craving for excitement, and this is most easily attained by stirring up the primitive instincts. The instincts for fighting enemies and hunting for prey are unsuitable for a civilised community, and find their natural

[1] Burt, Cyril, *The Listener*, Feb. 22nd, 1933, p. 296.

outlet in playing games. Boxing, football, cricket and other forms of sport involve rivalry, and spring more or less directly from the instinct of pugnacity. Travelling and sight-seeing arise from the instinct of wandering, while the instinct of self-display finds satisfaction in dress and the cultivation of social graces. The cinema and the theatre, the dance hall and the music hall, gently stimulate the sex instinct, while much of the pleasure of visiting football matches and cinemas, and of parading the park and the streets, is due to its stimulation of the gregarious instinct. Betting and gambling partly depend on the forcible excitement of the acquisitive instinct. Hence the majority of our leisure occupations fulfil, in an artificial and imaginary form, the desires which cannot be gratified during working hours. It might be thought that they lead to the formation of a frivolous and pleasure-seeking community, but Prof. Burt maintains that if the instincts are there, it is better for them to find some harmless outlet than to be summarily repressed.

Leisure and Temperance.—It might be thought that the increased leisure of the working classes as compared with pre-war times would result in more time being spent at public-houses, and an increase of intemperance. So far from this having happened, there is no doubt whatever that the sobriety of the nation has greatly improved. The sample statistics adduced[1] show that in 1929 the convictions for drunkenness in England and Wales were only

Year.	Convictions for drunkenness.		Deaths from cirrhosis.		Other deaths with record of alcohol.		Millions of gallons of alcohol consumed.	
	Men.	Women.	Men.	Women.	Men.	Women.	United Kingdom.	Great Britain.
1913	153,112	35,765	2,264	1,732	1,112	719	92	84·5
1918	21,853	7,222	1,121	609	222	74	37	—
1929	43,536	8,430	1,174	604	401	173	—	50·5

[1] *Cf., The Alliance Year Book*, 1931, p. 328.

about a fourth as numerous as in 1913. However, they were nearly twice as many as those observed in 1918, when the shortage of alcoholic liquor reached its most acute stage, so there is plenty of room for improvement. The deaths from cirrhosis of the liver—which is due in the majority of cases to excessive indulgence in alcohol—ran more or less parallel to the convictions for drunkenness, and so did other deaths with a record of alcoholism. The actual consumption of alcohol is recorded in terms of millions of gallons of absolute alcohol, and it will be seen that it was only about three-fifths as great in 1929 as in 1913, though half as great again as in 1918.

The improvement in sobriety is due in part to the rival attractions of the cinema, to an increase of self-respect, and to the force of public opinion, but the most important cause of all is undoubtedly the huge increase in the taxation of alcoholic liquors. This is so great that in 1929 the per capita consumption of beer and spirits was less than half as great as in 1912–13, though the expenditure was nearly twice as great. As can be seen from the sample data adduced,[1] the expenditure was substantially greater in 1929 than in pre-war times, even when due allowance is made for the increased cost of living. It therefore follows that if taxation were reduced to its pre-war figure there would be a great increase of intemperance, though it is improbable that it would reach pre-war figures. As can be realised from the data in the table on page 175, the average man expends a certain proportion of his wages on alcoholic liquor, almost regardless of its cost. If liquor is cheap he is therefore apt to drink too much; if it is dear, he can seldom afford to do so.

Lack of employment, with its accompanying reduction of spending power, naturally curtails the expenditure to a marked degree. For instance, the licensing statistics[2]

[1] Vernon, H. M., *The Alcohol Problem*, London, 1928, p. 75 (with added information).
[2] *Nat. Temp. Quarterly*, No. 101, p. 281, 1934.

show that, in 1932, various towns such as Walsall, Smethwick and Burnley, where there is a great deal of unemployment, had only 3 to 4 per cent. the number of convictions for drunkenness as compared with those occurring in 1913, the actual proportion of convictions being 0·4 to 1·0 per 10,000 of the population. In contrast to this strikingly small rate, we find that in popular seaside resorts such as Blackpool and Brighton the convictions were 60 and 76 per cent. respectively on the 1913 convictions, the actual rate being 13·0 and 15·9 per 10,000 of the population.

Year.	Per capita consumption of			Per capita expenditure.	Cost of living.	Relative expenditure on alcohol.
	Beer.	Spirits.	Mean.			
1912–13 (U.K.)	100	100	100	100	100	100
1918 (U.K.) ...	36	48	42	158	203	78
1920 (U.K.) ...	75	69	72	279	249	112
1922 (U.K.) ...	58	53	55	208	183	114
1929 (Gt. Brit.)	59	40	49	181	164	109

THE BEST USE OF LEISURE

Everyone would admit that working men and women, after a hard day of dull but strenuous physical labour, are fully entitled to employ a part of their leisure hours in some such manner as a visit to the cinema, which makes no call on their physical activities, but acts as a mild mental stimulant and provokes pleasurable day-dreams. The clerk, employed all day on sedentary work in an office, is likewise fully entitled to indulge part of his leisure hours in physical exercise such as dancing or the vigorous playing of games. Again, both manual and black-coated workers spend a great deal of their time at home, listening to music and talks on the wireless. Some of the broadcasts are designedly educational, and form an increasingly valuable channel for instruction, but probably the great majority of listeners make but little use of the opportunities offered them. Yet pure recreations, involving no effort, inevitably pall if indulged in to excess, and a great deal more happiness in life would be attained if a portion of the leisure time were expended on some useful pursuit, or on education.

Useful Work in the Home.—The great majority of working-class women are called upon to expend a good deal of their leisure time on useful work at home. In past times the wife of a working man spent almost the whole of her time in unending toil about the house, especially so if she had young children to bring up; but nowadays, owing to the introduction of labour-saving devices such as gas-cookers and electric light, and the partial substitution of tinned and other ready-cooked foods for home cooking, her essential labours are lightened a good deal, and she has sufficient leisure to enable her to visit the cinema, and perhaps to undertake extra work at home such as dressmaking. The husband, who has usually been working at a factory all day, may be too tired to undertake much additional manual labour, but frequently he is able to put in an hour or two of work in a garden or allotment, if he has one. Thereby he obtains, not only fresh air, but a welcome addition of food to the family resources.

In order that working-class men and women may be stimulated to devote their leisure time to the maintenance of a high standard of comfort and cleanliness in their homes, it is necessary, first and foremost, that they should be enabled to occupy fair-sized and well-appointed dwellings at a reasonable rent, compatible with their resources. Unfortunately this is what large numbers of them are quite unable to do. There was a tremendous shortage of houses everywhere after the war, and strenuous efforts were made by the Government and by local authorities to overtake it. It can be seen from the statistical data adduced[1] that between 1919 and 1929 nearly 1,500,000 dwellings were built in England and Wales, and 100,000 in Scotland. Of the dwellings in

DWELLINGS BUILT BETWEEN 1919 AND 1929.

Date.	Number of dwellings built:	
	England and Wales.	Scotland.
1919–22	251,983	{ 26,169 from 1920–23
1923	86,215	
1924	136,889	5,949
1925	173,426	10,054
1926	217,629	15,446
1927	238,914	22,175
1928	169,532	20,243
1929	202,060	—
Total ...	1,476,648	100,036

England and Wales, 537,618 were built by private enterprise unassisted by subsidies, and the remainder with the aid of State subsidies. In the year ending September, 1933, the rate of building was higher than in any previous year but 1927, as 218,313 houses were built in England and Wales.[2] But all this building has proved insufficient to fill the gap, and as many of the houses were built for sale while most of the remainder are too highly rented for any but well-to-do artisans, the ill-paid workers are not much better off than they were before the war. It was stated by the Minister of Health, in the spring of 1933,[3] that the number of low-rented houses (at inclusive rents

[1] Cf. *Housing Policy in Europe*, I.L.O., Geneva, 1930, p. 67.
[2] *The Times*, Nov. 10th, 1933.
[3] L.c.

of 10s. a week or less) has been increased by only 13 per cent. since 1918, and the *Architects' Journal*, as the result of a special survey, estimated that approximately 1,400,000 houses of this class are still required for housing and re-housing the poorer wage-earners.

The terrible state of overcrowding in London is illustrated by the census returns for 1921.[1]

PERSONS PER ROOM IN THE COUNTY OF LONDON.

Living more than:	1911. Persons.	1921. Persons.	Increase (+) or decrease (—)	
			Persons	Ratio. Per cent.
2 persons per room	758,786	683,498	—75,288	—9·9
3 ,, ,, ,,	173,637	147,591	—26,046	—15·0
4 ,, ,, ,,	38,346	30,904	—7,442	—19·4
5 ,, ,, ,,	8,903	6,711	—2,192	—24·6
6 ,, ,, ,,	2,349	1,968	—381	—16·2
7 ,, ,, ,,	575	768	+193	+33·6
8 ,, ,, ,,	159	376	+217	+136·5
9 ,, ,, ,,	42	250	+208	
10 ,, ,, ,,	12	160	+148	
11 ,, ,, ,,	12	50	+38	
12 ,, ,, ,,	0	26	+26	

This table shows that in 1921 nearly 700,000 persons were living more than 2 per room, and 150,000 more than 3 per room. These numbers show an improvement on the 1911 census figures, but gross overcrowding, where 8 or more persons were occupying a single room, was worse in 1921 than in 1911. We see that in a few instances there were 12 or 13 persons per room. Taking the country as a whole, it was found that, in 1921 the number of persons living in dwellings with more than 2 persons per room was slightly less than in 1911; but the returns of the 1931 census, so far as they are issued, indicate that the relation of dwellings to families was no

[1] *Cf.* Report No. 2253 of the London County Council, p. 12.

better in 1931 than in 1921.[1] All the efforts made have only just kept pace with the increasing number of families, and have done little to wipe off the war shortage.

The Government has recently brought forward a scheme of slum clearance under which the local authorities all over the country have submitted programmes contemplating the erection of over 200,000 new houses in the next five years. In the London area, where the problem is a much larger one than in any other centre, a programme has been advanced by the London County Council for the displacement and re-housing of 250,000 persons during the next ten years, at an expenditure of about £35,000,000.[2] Unfortunately these clearance plans, welcome as they are, do nothing to meet the shortage of low-rented houses, and it is to be hoped that they will be supplemented by a vigorous policy of building additional houses of this character. Indeed, it has been strenuously maintained[3] that the overcrowding ought to be dealt with first by the provision of suitable alternative accommodation, and that " till this has been done it will be impossible to make a beginning either of slum-clearance schemes or of the improvement of the existing houses." In a recent debate in Parliament[4] it was stated that in the next five years 465,000 new houses would be provided by the Wheatley subsidy, the 1930 Act, or private enterprise, but that this number would do little to fill the gap, for the *Economist* estimated that 300,000 additional families would be requiring accommodation. It was accordingly suggested that a National Housing Corporation should be formed, which would be able to act where local authorities and private enterprise failed.

It will be realised that if the manual worker has a

[1] Unwin, R., *The Listener*, Mar. 29th, 1933, p. 473.
[2] L.C.C. " Housing No. 30," July 25th, 1933.
[3] Simon, E. D., *How to Abolish the Slums*, London, 1929, p. 61; *cf. The Anti-Slum Campaign*, London, 1933.
[4] *Cf. The Times*, Dec. 13th, 1933.

comfortable, well-built and well-furnished home, in which he can take a genuine pride, he is much more likely to stay at home in the evenings and occupy himself with small household jobs, listening-in, hobbies, reading and self-education, than if he is compelled to put up with a miserable and overcrowded hovel. He is perforce driven into the streets, and drifts thence to the public-house, where he finds warmth, light and congenial company. The wife, if she has a pleasant home, feels the joy of it and the self-respect which it entails even more than the husband, since she is seldom absent from it for more than a few minutes at a time. The children can likewise stay comfortably indoors if they wish to do so, instead of having to play in the streets.

The provision of gardens and allotments in urban areas is often difficult and sometimes impossible, but there can be no doubt that in most areas allotment schemes could be developed on a much larger scale than those now existing. In 1923 there were 1,086,688 allotments provided in England and Wales, with a total area of 87,000 acres. Half of these allotments were provided by Local Authorities and a tenth of them by the Railways. The remainder were provided by private effort.[1] In Scotland there were 27,976 allotments, with a total area of 1,622 acres.

Education.—The educational facilities available for those members of the wage-earning classes who wish to profit by them are already very considerable, and they can be increased without much difficulty whenever the demand justifies it. It is pointed out[2] that in 1924 the Workers' Educational Association had about 20,000 members, of whom 7,000 were working in three-year tutorial classes and 12,000 in one-year preparatory classes. The Workers' Educational Trade Union Committee arranges special

---

[1] *Internat. Lab. Rev.*, 10, p. 86, 1924.
[2] C.O.P.E.C. Commission Reports, Vol. II, p. 154, 1924.

facilities for trade union members on W.E.A. lines. The adult schools number about 50,000 members, with an average weekly attendance of 30,000, while there are fifteen educational settlements, with a student membership of about 5,000. There are several Working People's Colleges at which students take residential courses lasting for a period ranging from a single term to two years. There are University Extra-mural Departments, providing extension lectures and university tutorial classes; also the Co-operative Education Committee. The Young Men's Christian Association and the numerous Women's Institutes all over the country provide lectures and other educational facilities, but it is pointed out[1] that even if, at an outside estimate, 100,000 adults are engaged in more or less regular educational pursuits, this number represents only a very small fraction of the 18,000,000 men and women who possess the parliamentary franchise.

Half a million children leave the elementary schools every year with very little probability that they will receive any further education, and it is suggested[2] that a national campaign for the furtherance of adult education ought to be undertaken. The Report of the Government Adult Education Committee which was published in 1919 recommended a ten years' programme, but not a tithe of its suggestions had (in 1924) been put into force. The Board of Education estimate for " adult education " in 1923–24 was only £20,600, and the additional expenditure by local authorities may bring the total expenditure on this account to £50,000 at most. The raising of the school-leaving age is very important, since it would be likely to instil in the pupils a desire for further educational facilities, as well as helping to deal with juvenile unemployment. It is suggested[3] that the education received at school has not

[1] *L.c.* p. 157.
[2] *L.c.*
[3] Burns, C. D., *Leisure in the Modern World*, London, 1932, p. 159.

hitherto given men and women enough skill to use the leisure they already possess. Greater leisure must be accompanied by better education. Again, it is maintained[1] that most of us are disappointed bunglers in the art of life through sheer lack of knowledge and practice. The higher pleasures are acquired and cultivated tastes, and the coming generation must be taught how best to enjoy its increasing hours of freedom. A policy of "Secondary Education for All" has been expounded[2] which aims at the abolition of the distinction between the "elementary" education for the wage-earner and the "secondary" education for the black-coated worker, and thereby at bringing about a reduction of class-consciousness.

The educational influence of broadcasting cannot easily be estimated, but it is certainly substantial and it is bound to increase in the future. Already a thousand discussion groups have been formed in various parts of the country to listen to broadcast education talks, and the regular courses of lectures on economics, literature, history, languages, science, music, and other subjects offer ready opportunities to all for the acquirement of a smattering of knowledge, which should act as a stimulus to further reading and enquiry. There can, at the present day, be very few workers who are not within reach of a public library where they can get many if not most of the books they want, and a Central Library in London is now established as a clearing station from which genuine students can borrow the books which are too expensive or too little used to be stocked in most local libraries. Again, most towns have municipal classes for academic teaching, vocational instruction, and handicraft work.

Social Activities.—The more frivolous social activities, such as visits to cinemas and dance-halls, have already

[1] Burt, C., *The Listener*, Feb. 22nd, 1933, p. 296.
[2] Tawney, R. H., *Secondary Education for All: a Policy for Labour*, London.

been mentioned. The less frivolous activities include membership of clubs and similar organisations, where instruction is provided as well as amusements. An investigation in Bethnal Green showed that 28 per cent. of the boys and 33 per cent. of the girls belonged to some social organisation.[1] The Boy Scout and Girl Guide Associations are among the most important of such organisations, and the Bethnal Green Survey of Recreational Facilities showed that 34 per cent. of the children at the elementary schools belonged to them, or to the allied groups of "Cubs" and "Brownies." Of ex-elementary children between the ages of 14 and 18, 20 per cent. belonged to the former groups, while some of the older ones became "Rovers" and "Rangers."

An indication of the facilities offered for recreations and amusements in large towns is afforded by the information collected at Liverpool.[2] In 1930 the people, who number 880,000, were provided with 400 band performances in the public parks, and from 1,000 to 8,000 of them attended each performance. The recreation grounds include 89 cricket pitches, 172 football grounds, 400 tennis courts and 53 bowling greens, and it was estimated that the membership of the cricket clubs amounted to 6,000, of football clubs to 15,000, of tennis clubs to 10,000, and of bowls clubs to 4,000. The 11 closed and 5 open-air swimming baths had 2,257,000 attendances, or about three per head of the population. The public libraries contain 482,000 books, from which 4,000,000 books were issued per year. The art gallery had 234,000 attendances per year, and the museum 2,160 attendances daily.

The sporting activities mentioned were almost exclusively the domain of the men, for working-class women, after marriage and withdrawal from industry, are usually too much occupied with the cares of the home and

[1] *New Aspects of the Problem of Hours of Work*, p. 10, 1933.
[2] *L.c.* p. 11.

of their growing families to have time or inclination for games. Their relaxation is chiefly met by social intercourse with neighbours.

The women's institutes mentioned previously offer great attractions, especially for those living in the country. There are now more than five thousand institutes in existence, with more than a quarter of a million members.[1] The subscription is only 2s. a year, and the movement is very democratic, the squire's lady, the farmer's wife and the labourer's " missus " all being equal. The members club together to buy seed potatoes, fruit trees and other garden necessaries. They get guidance about fruit-bottling, jam-making, cooking, basket-making, rug-making. They pay a good deal of attention to the arts, such as music, folk-dancing, play-acting and art needlework. They help to build village halls, and see that their members are represented on such bodies as parish councils and the education and housing committees of the county councils.

An important side of social activity depends on travel. The modern movement for rambling and hiking takes small groups of young persons into the country, where they get open-air exercise under peaceful conditions and the opportunity of observing nature. In many parts of the country a number of inexpensive hostels are available for the hikers, as well as camping associations, and they can easily extend the range of their movements by the motor transport facilities which coach and bus offer in almost every direction. For those who can afford it, the Workers' Travel Association and other organisations arrange for cheap holidays at home and abroad.

[1] *Cf. The Listener*, Nov. 15th, 1933, p. 754.

LEISURE AND THE TWO-SHIFT SYSTEM

The widespread adoption of the two-shift system would have a considerable influence, not only on the leisure time available, but upon the manner in which it is utilised. We saw that, on the two-shift system as at present organised, the industrial worker averages only 41 hours a week instead of the 48 hours observed by most single-shift workers. This means that, not only are the hours of leisure substantially increased, but the workers are less tired by their labours and are the more ready to occupy their leisure by physical activities such as housework, outdoor games, gardening, etc., while they are more mentally alert and receptive if they desire education and instruction. It is true that the alteration in the hours of work and the weekly alternation of shifts are apt to throw additional work on the housewife in cooking meals. The mother of a family already has to get an early breakfast for her husband and a later one for her children, and if one of her daughters is on shift-work a still earlier breakfast is necessary in alternate weeks, coupled with the provision of a substantial meal on her return from work at about 2.30 p.m. Again, when she is on afternoon shift she needs a good meal at about 10.30 p.m., but there is no reason why the girl herself should not assist in getting these extra meals, or, if they are undertaken by the mother, in doing some other housework in compensation.

Shift-workers are free for the greater part of the mornings and afternoons in alternate weeks, and can therefore get daylight open-air exercise at all times of the year. The single-shift workers have no opportunity of such exercise in the winter months, as it is dark when they go to work in the morning, and dark when they return in the afternoon. Two-shift workers could, therefore, arrange to play outdoor games—to be held both in the mornings and the afternoons—much more easily than single-shift workers, and they would tend to substitute this more healthy form of exercise for the evening dances attended by many of the single-shift workers. They would not be cut off from such dances altogether, as they would always have their Saturday evenings free, and every evening in alternate weeks. Entertainments such as cinemas at present begin at mid-day or later, and would not, therefore, be available for the afternoon shift, but if there were enough demand it would be easy to open them at 10 or 11 a.m., and render them accessible for these shift-workers. Such morning attendances would help to relieve the congestion which is usually experienced in the evenings. Clubs and educational classes have hitherto been mostly arranged for evening attendances, but the morning attendances could be arranged for if there was a sufficient demand. The workers attending morning classes, unfatigued by preceding manual work, would be much more likely to profit by them than the tired workers who attend in the evenings.

If the mother of the family is herself on shift-work there can be no doubt that she is better circumstanced than when on day-work. She not only has more leisure for attending to household duties, but she sees much more of her family. When she is on the afternoon shift she can prepare the mid-day dinner for her children and husband, and when on the morning shift she sees a great deal of them in the afternoon and evening. When on single-shift, however, she is cut off from them between the hours of 7.30 a.m. and 5.30 p.m.—except, perhaps, for a short interval at mid-day—and she is more tired by her longer hours of work. Of course it is not at all desirable that a woman who has to run a home should undertake industrial work at all, even if she has no children, but the fact remains that many of them do so, especially in the textile trades.

LEISURE AND THE UNEMPLOYED

However desirable it is that employed workers should occupy their leisure to the best advantage, the problem is immensely more important for unemployed workers. At the present time considerably over two million unemployed workers are registered at the employment exchanges, and though their numbers are happily undergoing a gradual diminution, it seems probable that it will be some years before they are reduced to pre-war figures, even if they ever attain them. Some of the unemployed have been unable to obtain any work for years, and youths of 18 or 20 may never have done a day's work since they left school. Such widespread and persistent unemployment inevitably causes moral and spiritual deterioration as well as physical enfeeblement, and is one of the greatest tragedies of the modern state. It might, therefore, be expected that the Government would themselves attempt to alleviate it, and they have done so to some extent by extending benefits under the Unemployment Insurance Scheme. The Ministry of Labour co-operates with the National Council of Social Service in fostering the voluntary movement for the welfare and occupational training of the unemployed. In March, 1934, 250,000 men and women were availing themselves of the facilities offered.[1] Also the new Unemployment Bill now being considered in Parliament is providing for the maintenance of training courses for the unemployed, both men and women, but one member maintained[2] that the Government proposals " would not touch the fringe of the great problem of dealing adequately with the thousands of young men and women who were virtually running riot as a direct consequence of being unable to find work."

One of the most successful of the many private efforts is that undertaken by the Society of Friends.[3] Relief work

[1] *The Times*, Apr. 12th, 1934
[2] *L.c.* Feb. 21st, 1934.
[3] Details taken from pamphlet issued by the Friends' Allotment Committee, Friends' House, Euston Road, London, N.W.1, 1933.

was started in the South Wales coalfields in 1926 by the provision of seeds, etc., for allotments at very reduced prices. This work was subsequently assisted through the Lord Mayor's fund (1929–30) and by a Government grant (1930–31), so that by the end of 1931 over 64,000 men throughout England and Wales were being assisted to grow fresh food, which was valued at £400,000. The scheme offers to every unemployed, partially employed, or seriously impoverished worker the seed potatoes, vegetable seeds, fertilisers and tools requisite for planting a plot of 300 square yards. The men group themselves into societies which afford opportunities for mutual help and co-operation. The officers of these societies, now numbering over 2,200, collect the contributions from the men to pay for their portion of the cost of the supplies.

During the 1932–33 season the Government offered a grant up to £12,500 for the extension of the scheme, and it was necessary to bring the number of men helped up to 100,000 in order to qualify for the grant. A grant of £15,000 has now been offered on condition that private subscriptions are raised, and if 200,000 are helped it is estimated that of the total of £80,000 required the men themselves will contribute £45,000, the Government £15,000, and private subscriptions £20,000. It is difficult to visualise a better and more economical scheme than this. The pity is that it is not extended greatly by means of a more generous Government grant.

The Society of Friends are, in addition, convinced of the necessity for developing schemes of land settlement, and ask for a further sum of £10,000 for this purpose. They realise that their present schemes touch only tens of thousands among the millions of unemployed, but they have within them the possibilities of development towards a large measure of self-help and independence, as well as the removal of depression through idleness.

Numerous smaller schemes for the development of

allotment and other clubs have been gradually growing up all over the country, and the British Broadcasting Corporation has given the movement welcome support through the help of their special commissioner, Mr. S. P. B. Mais. Mr. Mais has toured all over the country, and, by a series of broadcast talks, subsequently published in *The Listener* and in book form,[1] has revealed to the British public both the magnitude of the task and the efforts being made to meet it. He considers that allotment schemes form one of the best methods of combating unemployment, and in Sheffield, for instance, he found 1,800 allotments being worked by cutlers, moulders, file-makers and other out-of-work metal-workers. It is to be regretted that the starting of an allotment club appears to be by no means easy in many localities. The unemployed have sunk into a state of apathy from which it is difficult to arouse them. In Stirling, for instance, 100 out of the 243 free plots available were lying idle, in spite of the 2,000 unemployed in the district. At Brighton there were 6,000 to 7,000 unemployed, few, if any, of them working on allotments. It needs men of very vigorous personality to get the unemployed men together and start a scheme of work. Fortunately such men were found at many centres, and were willing to devote themselves voluntarily to setting the clubs in motion.

Clubs for carpentry, boot-repairing and other small repairing jobs were being formed at a number of centres. The usual method of procedure was to collect a small group of men and set them to work in some disused room, or if one was not available to get the men to build a room for themselves. Usually the club was entirely run by the men and sometimes it blossomed out into good-sized workshops, fitted with lathes and other machinery. It was found that men who had no previous experience of the work

[1] Mais, S. P. B., *The Listener*, Jan. 23rd, 1933, *et seq.*; also *S.O.S. Talks on Unemployment*, London, 1933.

speedily became highly skilled at it, and developed a keen interest and pride in the articles they produced. In country districts these might consist largely of wheelbarrows, ladders, chicken coops and meat safes, and in urban districts, of chairs, mangles, toys. Some of the clubs had classes for languages and literature, but education was not sought for as a rule. In Liverpool there were five Juvenile Instruction centres, attended by a quarter of the 5,000 juvenile unemployed. At the Central Technical School provision was made for unemployed youths of 16 to 18.

In some rural areas the men were put to work on fencing, ditching, hedging, and lopping trees for firewood. In others they made roads, footpaths and recreation grounds. The Oxfordshire County Council provided a grant to enable 100 men to receive 40 hours' free instruction in woodwork, and wood to the value of 10s. for each man. Physical training classes were started in addition. It was calculated that, taking the country as a whole, some 150,000 men were using the clubs. As the Master of Balliol College, Oxford, said,[1] " There is no lack of uneconomic work to be done, and the beauty of it is that the doing of it restores the worker's self-respect, gives him an honoured place in the community, pride in craftsmanship, the energy, joviality, and sense of comradeship that are the hall-mark of all good workmen."

The unemployed women were being catered for to some extent as well as the men. In Durham and Northumberland many of the women were eager to go into service, and 7,000 girls from the distressed areas had found jobs in the last four years. The Ministry of Labour was running 33 training centres, and was providing a further supply of 5,000 girls a year. The wives of the unemployed had clubs in a few districts, where they did needlework, had singing classes and discussion groups, while in Sunderland

[1] *The Listener*, Mar. 15th, 1933, p. 415.

there was a scheme of " Keep Fit " classes for women and girls. Some distressed areas had girls' clubs for dressmaking, cookery and dancing. Others had emergency open-air nurseries where children of two to five could be kept all day.

A council of six universities has organised summer camps for unemployed men, and in the present year (1934) ten camps are to be run,[1] each accommodating a hundred unemployed men and a staff of fifteen university men. So far as possible the work done does not encroach on ordinary paid labour. For instance, in one site a bathing plunge was constructed, after the ground had been cleared of trees and undergrowth ; at another, the ground is to be cleared for an archæological survey. After the morning's work there are games, and in the evenings there are hobbies to suit all tastes, from wood-carving and toy-making to the drama and camp-fire sing-songs. The camp life causes the spirit of the men to be renewed and their health to be improved, and they return home with a fresh interest in life. The camps destroy the idea of class division. Everything is exactly the same for everyone, the university men joining the others in their work and in their games.

HOW OTHER COUNTRIES MEET THE PROBLEM OF LEISURE

The problem of leisure has been considered much more seriously and thoroughly by several other countries than by our own, and in some of them it is officially supervised by the Government. Such official control is wholly alien to the spirit of this country, where the mere fact of compulsion or semi-compulsion would be considered to rob any scheme for occupying leisure hours of its essential attribute of freedom of choice. Nevertheless, we can

[1] *The Observer*, Feb. 25th, 1934.

learn a good deal from some of these official schemes, and apply what is best in them on a private and voluntary basis.

Italy.—It is probable that the best organised of all the schemes developed in foreign countries is the *Opera Nazionale Dopolavoro*, the National Institute for the Use of Leisure, which was established by the Fascist State in Italy about eight years ago. It had a membership of 280,000 in 1926, and one of 1½ millions at the beginning of 1930.[1] The Institute deals with the problems of welfare, education and recreation of the working classes. It is stated[2] that, " These tasks have become an integral part of the State's activities, and in this field also the State asserts its position as the controlling force of the nation." The activities of the Institute are classed under four principal headings (*a*) Instruction, or culture for the people and the teaching of trades ; (*b*) Artistic education, such as dramatic societies, music and chorus-singing, cinematography, wireless, and folklore ; (*c*) Physical education (including the Italian Excursion Federation and the Central Sporting Commission) ; (*d*) Social welfare and hygiene, dealing with dwellings, provision for the future, and leisure-time occupation for the various classes of workmen.[3] The instruction programme includes libraries, reading-rooms, evening instruction and people's universities. Sport includes gymnastics, fencing, swimming, rowing, cycling, running and recreations such as Sunday excursions, tours of pleasure and instruction, pilgrimages to battlefields. There are practical courses to encourage the cultivation of allotments and gardens, and the formation of depots for the sale of foodstuffs.

The Institute has a network of provincial and local branches all over the country, and there are in addition

Annual Review, I.L.O., Geneva, 1931.
[2] Hamilton, Cicely, *Modern Italy*, London, 1932, p. 221.
L.c.

THE PROBLEM OF LEISURE

special organisations such as women's *Dopolavoro*, a rural *Dopolavoro* and a railway *Dopolavoro*.

Germany.—This country has followed Italy in founding a *Nach der Arbeit*, or " After Working Hours " organisation which is admittedly copied from the *Dopolavoro* Institute. The " N.D.A." aims at dedicating " the largest and most beautiful building in each town " to the workers as their " House of Labour,"[1] and it intends to make the best films, the best plays, the best music, the best entertainments of all kinds available free of cost to any worker who wishes to take advantage of them. The cost will be met out of the seized trade union funds, or by the State itself. Open-air theatres are planned, while travelling motor film vans will visit lonely country districts. Camps will be formed, where the workers can have physical training in an atmosphere of comradeship. In addition to week-end tours there will be annual holiday tours, and it is hoped that an adequate annual holiday will be arranged for every German worker. The scheme is to be inspired by the Nazi ideal of a national community without class barriers. The clerk and the employer will be able to avail themselves of the Houses of Labour no less than the manual worker. Every producer is regarded as a member of the State as distinct from a mere citizen, and Dr. Goebbels maintains[2] that " A State which is really bound up and identical with the people can never leave the people to itself."

It is to be remembered that this new organisation is not yet in working order, but it received its statutes at a meeting held in Berlin on November 27th, 1933,[3] and there can be little doubt that many of its activities will soon be well established. In Berlin it is expected that the fine building where the Prussian Diet sat is to be transferred to club uses.

[1] *The Times*, Nov. 25th, 1933.
[2] *L.c.* Dec. 2nd, 1933.
[3] *L.c.* Nov. 28th, 1933.

Sweden.—In Sweden the intellectual and physical education of the people has long been considered a matter mainly incumbent on the authorities. The Riksdag allocated 610,000 kr. for sport and sporting clubs in 1923–24, the municipalities likewise voted much money, and the Workers' Educational Association gave 233,000 kr. out of members' contributions.[1] Sport has rapidly spread among the younger workers, football being the most popular summer sport, and ski-ing the winter one. Swedish gymnastics are adopted in schools, but not as a national sport. Women indulge mostly in walking expeditions and gymnastic clubs. In 1923 there were 1,200 societies, with 140,000 members, affiliated to the National Federation of Swedish Gymnastic and Sports Societies. The intense rivalry of the societies often leads to an excessive devotion to sport, and an employer remarked, " The best man on the football ground is very seldom the best in the workshop."

The W.E.A. had a membership of over 500,000 in 1923. Most of its work is effected by libraries, lectures and study circles, and in 1922–23 there were 1,638 circles with 21,687 members.[2] The employers assist in organising courses of lectures and libraries, while many of the members of the National Federation of Trade Unions take an active part in the study circle movement.

The allotment movement is developing successfully. There were over 30,000 allotments in 1922, and half of the 6,640 allotments at Stockholm are now provided with well-built cottages, in which the owners and their families live during the summer season. Many of these cottages are owned by clerks and artisans, and are not limited to the well-to-do classes.

Czecho-Slovakia.—This country has a number of large societies for the encouragement of sport and education. In 1922 the gymnastic societies had a membership of

---

[1] *Internat. Lab. Rev.*, 9, p. 227, 1924.
[2] *L.c.* 9, p. 879.

500,000, and the Labour Academy (for workers' education, holiday camps, etc.) had 250,000 members. An Educational Union had 96 musical clubs, 124 choral societies, 484 dramatic societies, and 369 branches owning libraries. The lantern lectures given numbered 15,000.

Austria.—In this country an organisation of worker-tourists called "Die Naturfreunde" has been formed. In 1923 it had 1,308 local branches with 180,000 members, of whom 78,000 were in Austria, and the remainder in Germany, Switzerland, and other countries.[1] There were 370,000 allotment-holders in Vienna in 1922, or 50 per cent. more than in 1920.

Other Countries.—Information about several other countries is recorded in the *International Labour Review* for 1924. In Belgium the Provincial Councils of various large towns appointed committees in 1919–20 to consider what the workers should do with their spare time, and to discover wholesome forms of recreation for them. The Hainault Committee expended large sums of money on physical, artistic, intellectual, and moral training, and smaller sums on allotments and housing.

In Finland the State has made large grants to encourage the work of public utility societies, state libraries, gymnastic and sports societies, workers' institutes, study circles, domestic schools and dramatic societies. The Workers' Athletic Association had 25,360 adult members in 1923.[2]

It is stated that in Russia sports and games, the cinema and the radio are all organised centrally by the Communist party.

GENERAL CONCLUSIONS

The brief account given above makes no pretence to completeness, but it is sufficient to show that in several

[1] *L.c.* p. 227.
[2] *L.c.* p. 573.

countries the problem of leisure is being considered with the serious attention it undoubtedly deserves. It is to be hoped that in our own country leisure will gradually become better organised, more or less on the lines of voluntary efforts which have already proved fairly successful. The State might well assist the movement by liberal grants of money, provided that it did not lay down rigid rules for their application. Naturally it would have to be convinced that the money was not being ill-spent, but that need not involve autocratic dictation on its part.

The unemployment problem is always likely to be with us to a greater or less extent, for even in the pre-war times of good trade the number of unemployed never fell below 200,000,[1] and when trade was neither particularly good nor particularly bad it was in the neighbourhood of 500,000. A small pool of unemployed persons is essential, as there are bound to be fluctuations in all industries, and if no extra supply of labour is available it would be impossible to expand an industry when it was desired to do so. Though the provision of opportunities for exercising useful leisure occupations is of increasing importance among the employed as their hours of work are reduced, it is of still greater importance among the unemployed, so much so that this provision ought to be considered an absolute obligation on the State. It must be admitted that we have far to travel from our present position before we reach or even approach this goal.

[1] *Britain's Industrial Future*, p. 271, 1928.

INDEX

AGRICULTURAL labourers, health of, 130; and two-shift system, 166
Agriculture, hours of work in, 49
Alcohol, consumption of in relation to leisure, 173-175
Allotments, and leisure, 176, 180; and unemployed, 188, 189
America, unemployment in, 5, 14; increasing productivity in, 15, 16, 38; standardisation in, 29; five-day week in, 59; National Recovery Administration, 68, 69; two-shift system in, 142
Amusements, in leisure hours, 170-172, 183
Artificial silk, and two-shift system, 100-102

BAKING, hours of work in, 51, 53
Benefit, unemployment, 61, 62
Boys, under two-shift system, 142-144
Breakfast, of shift workers, 120, 125
British Broadcasting Corporation, and unemployment clubs, 189
Broadcasting, and education, 176, 182
Building trade, hours of work in, 47

CAMPS, for unemployed, 191
Canning industry, and two-shift system, 132, 133
Catering trade, hours of work in, 50-52
Census, of persons per room in London houses, 178
Chain work, 25
Cinema trade, hours of work in, 53

Cloakrooms, under two-shift Orders, 82, 83
Coal mining, hours of work in, 55
Combinations, industrial, 32, 33
Comparative mortality rate of industrial workers, 129, 130
Continuous industries, and shifts, 63
Convention on hours of work, 65, 66
Cost of living, changes in, 175
Cost of production, 71; and 40-hour week, 65, 70

DEBATES, parliamentary, on two-shift system, 137, 141, 154-159, 161-164
Differential piece rate, 25
Digestion, influence of shift work on, 119
Direct labour costs, 71, 76
Displacement of labour, and rationalisation, 37-41
Distribution of goods, organised, 34
Distributive trades, hours of work in, 52
Dwellings, built and building, 177-179

ECONOMIC depression, and reduced hours of work, 60
Education, in leisure hours, 170-172, 180-182; and broadcasting, 182; and two-shift system, 185, 186
Employers, and reduced hours of work, 65-67, 75, 76; and National Recovery Act in America, 69; and two-shift system, 80-82, 92-94
Employment, exchanges, 6; and productivity, 17; and purchasing power, 36; and rationalisation, 37, 38; and

197

insured workers, 41-43; and reduced hours of work, 60-64, 66; of women, 77 *et seq.*; extra, caused by two-shift system, 90, 91

Engineering industries, and two-shift system, 102, 104, 139

Export markets, and reduced hours of work, 67

FACTORY and Workshops Act, 134

Faintness, of shift workers, 120, 124

Fatigue, caused by overtime work, 135, 136

Five-day week, 56-60

Food, taken by shift workers, 120, 125; production of under two-shift system, 103, 132, 139; canning, and two-shift system, 133

Forty-hour week, 58, 59, 62, 63, 64-69; and overhead costs, 70, 75

Four-shift system, 63

Friends, Society of, and unemployment, 187, 188

Fruit-canning, and two-shift system, 132, 133; and overtime, 134

GAMES, during leisure hours, 171; and two-shift system, 185

Germany, unemployment in, 5, 9; increasing productivity in, 18; standardisation in, 29; two-shift system in, 141; utilisation of leisure in, 193

Great Britain, unemployment in, 6-9; increasing productivity in, 16; standardisation in, 28, 30; insured workers in, 41-43

HABIT, and preference for two-shift system, 148

Handwork, industries dependent on, 112

Health, influence of shift work on, 117-121; 127-131

Heating of factories under two-shift system, 145

Heavy industries, combinations in, 33

Home, work in, during leisure 170, 176

Hours of work, weekly, changes in, 44, 45; in individual industries, 46-49; in unregulated occupations, 50-53; in foreign countries, 53-55; and five-day week, 56; under two-shift Orders, 94-98, 107; abbreviated, 95, 96; exceptional, 97, 98; their influence on rate of production, 109-114; maximum under Factory Act, 134

Housework, done by shift workers, 126, 127

Housing shortage, 176-180

INCENTIVES to production, 32

Increase in hours of work, 45, 49

Industrial combinations, 32, 33

Industrial psychology, 27

Industries, various, unemployment in, 8; short time in, 11, 13; two-shift system in, 100-103, 134, 138-140; dependent on hand work, 112; dependent on machinery, 113

Instincts, and leisure occupations, 172, 173

Institutes, men's, 181, 192, 193; women's, 181, 184

Insurance statistics, unemployment, 6

Insured workers, changes in, 41-43

Intemperance, and leisure, 173-175

Intermittent employment, seasonal, 132-135; non-seasonal, 136

International Labour Conference, and hours of work, 65, 66, 70

Italy, utilisation of leisure in, 192

JUVENILES, unemployment of, 3; raising school age of, 4, 181; instruction centres for, 190

KRÜMPER system of rotation, 61

INDEX

LABOUR, increasing productivity of, 14-18; turnover, and two-shift system, 151, 152
Leisure, from working forty-hour week, 59; for arts and crafts, 167, 168; education for, 168; occupations during, 168-172; and instincts, 172, 173; and temperance, 173-175; best use of, 175-184; and work in home, 176; and education, 180-182; and social activities, 182-184; and two-shift system, 185, 186; and the unemployed, 187-191; utilisation of in Italy, 192, in Germany, 193, in Sweden, 194, in other countries, 194, 195
Libraries, for education, 182, 183
Lighting, under two-shift system, 144
Loss of working time, under two-shift system, 107-109

MANAGEMENT, scientific, 23-26
Managers, opinions of on two-shift system, 153
Mass production, 30-32
Masses, production for the, 31
Meal break, on two-shift system, 95, 96
Meals, of shift workers, 124-126
Messrooms, under two-shift Orders, 82, 83
Metal industries, and two-shift system, 102, 139
Monotony, and rest pauses, 58
Mortality rate, of workers on three-shift system, 129, 130
Motion study, 24
Motor-car industry, 16, 30, 31; and five-day week, 59
Munition workers, hours of work among, 110, 111

NATIONAL Recovery Administration, in America, 68, 69

OCCUPATIONS, using two-shift system, 100-103, 132, 138-140; in leisure hours, 168, 170-173
Opinions on two-shift system, of workers, 146-151; of managers, 153; of parents, 154, 155
Orders, two-shift, procedures adopted, 80-82; abuses in obtaining, 81; provisions of, 82; and welfare, 83; and transport, 83, 86; numbers granted, 86-88; workers involved, 89-91; reasons for obtaining, 92-94; hours of work under, 94-98; administration of when used intermittently, 137; permanent and temporary, 138; occupations concerned, 138-140; and boys, 142-144; and trade unions, 156-159; and joint industrial councils, 158; renewal of Act relating to, 161
Organisations of workers, and two-shift system, 156-160; and education, 180-181; and social activities, 183, 184; and the unemployed, 187-195
Output, and rationalisation, 37, 38; and rest pauses, 58; and five-day week, 60; effect of shift system on, 104-106
Overcrowding, in London, 178
Overhead costs, 70-73, 75, 76, 94, 141
Overtime work, in distributive trades, 52; and two-shift system, 133-135; and fatigue, 135, 136

PARENTS, opinions of on two-shift system, 154, 155
Parliament, debates on two-shift system in, 137, 141, 154-159, 161-164
Piece rate, differential, 25; group, 32
Planning and routing, 25
Potash industry, and production, 34
Production rate, under shift system, 104-106; with reduced hours of work, 109-114
Productivity of labour, increasing, 14-18; and employment, 17
Psychological tests for workers, 27

Public houses, resort to, and leisure, 173, 180

RATIONALISATION, defined, 19; its aims, 20-22; and scientific management, 23; and vocational selection, 26; and standardisation, 28; and mass production, 30; and industrial combinations, 32; and displacement of workers, 34; and technocracy, 35; and changes of employment, 37-41
Recreations, in leisure hours, 170-173, 175-184
Reduction in hours of work, 45; and five-day week, 56, 59; temporary, 60; permanent, 64-69
Repetition work, 30
Rest pauses, during work spells, 57, 59
Rotation, of employment, 61, 62
Rural areas, and unemployed, 190

SCHOOL age, raising of, 4
Scientific management, 23-26
Season, and hours of work, in building trade, 47; in agriculture, 49
Seasonal employment, and two-shift system, 132-135
Selection tests, 27
Selling organisations, 34
Shift systems, 73-76
Short time, in Great Britain, 11; in Germany, 12; in America, 12, 13
Sickness, influence of shift work on, 117-121, 128
Silk, artificial, and two-shift system, 100-102
Simplified practice, 29
Six-hour shifts, 63
Skilled workers, replaced by unskilled, 40
Sleep, hours of in shift workers, 121-123
Sobriety, and leisure, 173; and cost of living, 174, 175
Social activities, and leisure, 170, 172, 182-184

Speed of production, under shift system, 104-106; with reduced hours of work, 109-112
Spreading available work, 60-64
Standardisation of articles, 28-30
Steel trusts, 34
Substitution of labour, and rationalisation, 39-41
Supervisors, welfare, and shift system, 117-121
Sweden, utilisation of leisure in, 194

TAYLOR, F. W., and scientific management, 23-26
Technocracy, 35-37
Tests, selection, 27
Textile industries, and two-shift system, 100, 139, 180; hours of work in, 134; trade unions of, and two-shift system, 156, 159, 160
Three-shift system, and health, 127-131
Time and motion study, 24
Time-keeping, under two-shift system, 108, 109
Trade Unions, unemployment statistics, 6; and two-shift system, 156-160
Transport, of goods, 35; under two-shift Orders, 83-86; of ordinary day-workers, 86
Travel, in leisure hours, 184
Tripartite Conference, on hours of work, 65
Trusts, horizontal, 33, 34
Turnover, labour, and two-shift system, 151, 152
Two-shift system, 77-166; bad effects of, 78; Orders required for, 80-82; transport under, 83-86; workers involved, 89-91; reasons for adopting, 92-94; and hours of work, 94-98; in continuous operation, 99-131; and textile industries, 100, metal and engineering industries, 100-102, miscellaneous industries, 103; effect of on output, 104-106; loss of working time under, 107-109; and wages, 115; and health,

117-121 ; and seasonal employment, 132, 133 ; and overtime, 133-135 ; and non-seasonal intermittent employment, 136; administration of when used intermittently, 137 ; in foreign countries, 140-142 ; and boys, 142-144 ; lighting of factories under, 144 ; heating and ventilation under, 145 ; opinions of workers on, 146-151 ; effect of habit on preference for, 148; and labour turnover, 151, 152 ; opinions of managers on, 153 ; opinions of parents, 154, 155 ; opinions of workers' organisations, 156-160 ; debates on in Parliament, 161-164 ; elasticity of, 165 ; and leisure, 185, 186

UNEMPLOYED workers, and utilisation of leisure, 187-191 ; and allotments, 188, 189 ; and camps, 191

Unemployment, due to rise in productivity of labour, 1 ; a curse, 2 ; saps moral strength, 3 ; causes under-nourishment, 3 ; juvenile, 3 ; in various countries, 5, 9 ; in Great Britain, 6-9 ; insurance statistics, 6, 41-43 ; permanent and temporary, 10 ; and rationalisation, 37-41 ; and reduced hours of work, 60-64 ; throughout the world, 66 ; reduction of by means of two-shift system, 90, 91 ; and use of leisure, 187-191 ; in pre-war times, 196

United States, *see* America

Unregulated occupations, hours of work in, 50-53

Unskilled workers, replace skilled, 40

VEGETABLE-CANNING, and two-shift system, 133

Ventilation of factories under two-shift system, 145

Vocational selection and training, 26-28

WAGES, for reduced hours of work, 1 ; and forty-hour week, 63, 64-68 ; paid to shift workers, 115, 116

Weekly hours of work, changes in, 44, 45 ; in individual industries, 46-49 ; in unregulated occupations, 50-53 ; in foreign countries, 53-55 ; and five-day week, 56

Welfare, and two-shift Orders, 83, 84 ; supervisors, and shift system, 117-121 ; of unemployed, 187

Women, employment of on two-shift system, 77-165 ; replace men in industry, 40, 160 ; better than men at monotonous work, 164 ; centres for unemployed, 190

Workers, opinions of on two-shift system, 146-151 ; organisations of, and opinions, 156-160

Workers' Educational Association, 180, 181 ; in Sweden, 194

Working time, loss of under two-shift system, 107-109

YOUNG persons, number of in relation to school age, 4 ; and psychological tests, 27 ; hours of work of in unregulated occupations, 50 ; and National Recovery Administration in America, 68, 69 ; employment of on two-shift system, 79

Youths, and two-shift system, 142-144

PRINTED IN GREAT BRITAIN BY
MACKAYS LIMITED, CHATHAM